Scenes of Reading

Writing About Women
Feminist Literary Studies

General Editor

Esther Labovitz
Pace University

Advisory Board

Marie Collins
Rutgers-Newark University

Doris Guilloton
New York University

Lila Hanft
Case Western Reserve University

Mark Hussey
Pace University

Helane Levine-Keating
Pace University

Vol. 24

PETER LANG
New York · Washington, D.C./Baltimore · Boston
Bern · Frankfurt am Main · Berlin · Vienna · Paris

Nancy Cervetti

Scenes of Reading

Transforming Romance in Brontë, Eliot, and Woolf

PETER LANG
New York · Washington, D.C./Baltimore · Boston
Bern · Frankfurt am Main · Berlin · Vienna · Paris

140872

Library of Congress Cataloging-in-Publication Data

Cervetti, Nancy.
Scenes of reading: transforming romance
in Brontë, Eliot, and Woolf / Nancy Cervetti.
p. cm. — (Writing about women; vol. 24)
Includes bibliographical references (p.   ).
1. English fiction—Women authors—History and criticism. 2. Women and
literature—England—History—19th century. 3. Women and literature—
England—History—19th century. 4. English fiction—19th century—History
and criticism. 5. Brontë, Charlotte, 1816–1855—Characters—Women.
6. Eliot, George, 1819–1880—Characters—Women. 7. Woolf, Virginia,
1882–1941—Characters—Women. 8. Books and reading in
literature. 9. Women—England—Books and reading.
10. Women in literature. I. Title. II. Series.
PR878.W6C47   823'.809352042—DC21   97-8513
ISBN 0-8204-3805-7
ISSN 1053-7937

Die Deutsche Bibliothek-CIP-Einheitsaufnahme

Cervetti, Nancy:
Scenes of reading: transforming romance in Brontë, Eliot, and Woolf /
Nancy Cervetti. –New York; Washington, D.C./Baltimore; Boston;
Bern; Frankfurt am Main; Berlin; Vienna; Paris: Lang.
(Writing about women; Vol. 24)
ISBN 0-8204-3805-7

For My Grandmother
Maria Madalena Deluca

Acknowledgments

Grateful acknowledgment is made to the following for permission to reprint previously published material:

A version of "The German Connection in George Eliot," by Nancy Cervetti, *George Eliot and Europe*, ed. by John Rignall (1997). Reprinted by permission of Scolar Press, Great Britain.

"In the Breeches, Petticoats, and Laughter of *Orlando*," by Nancy Cervetti, *Journal of Modern Literature* 20 (Winter 1996). Reprinted by permission.

Contents

Preface   xi

Introduction: Women and the Novel   1

1   The German Connection in George Eliot   11

2   Reading Maggie Reading   29

3   Voice and Visibility in Charlotte Brontë   49

4   Lucy Snowe and the Politics of Location   71

5   Virginia Woolf In Her Father's Library   89

6   Rachel's Voyage Out   109

7   In the Breeches, Petticoats and
Pleasures of *Orlando*   123

Epilogue   137

Notes   143
Bibliography   161
Index   171

Preface

This book combines biography, literature, and feminist and discourse theory to examine the radical critiques of patriarchal culture performed by *Jane Eyre*, *Villette*, *The Mill on the Floss*, *The Voyage Out* and *Orlando*. Representational rather than exceptional, Charlotte Brontë, George Eliot, and Virginia Woolf demonstrate the immensely valuable collaboration between women and the novel in analyzing images and transforming realities of romance. In place of the ancient and very political romance plot, these authors create a much larger imaginary field in which female heroines as well as readers can consider and experiment with other possibilities. Jane Eyre, Lucy Snowe, Maggie Tulliver, Rachel Vinrace, and Orlando are strikingly different from the swooning beauties of traditional romance as well as different from one another. What they share is a love of language and a desire for intellectual expression that takes precedence over marriage and motherhood.

Mikhail Bakhtin traces the romance plot back to the Greek novels of the second to the sixth centuries A.D., and while this deeply entrenched paradigm does not disappear in Brontë, Eliot, and Woolf, it does shrink, assuming a place alongside other patterns and events, at times becoming an object of satire or an obstacle in the way of the heroine's development. The experiences of reading and writing so profoundly important in the lives of the authors repeat themselves in the lives of the heroines. Brontë, Eliot, and Woolf reveal a kind of agency in these scenes of reading. This intimate relation between women and language becomes a dynamic partnership providing the power to see beyond the narrow confines of a Thornfield Hall or a St. Ogg's. Through reading widely in a number of disciplines, the authors and their heroines hear the contradictions in any one point of view, contact multiple perspectives, and begin to engender and legitimize a variety of female images and voices outside those of wife and mother.

In reassessing these novels, in contrast to many cultural critics, I do not use contemporary theory to identify what they lack, what they silence or fail to say, or how they participate in the imperialist project. While this is important work, my focus is on what the novels do in a positive feminist way. At the same time, my intent is not to recreate a romantic ideology of the individual, but to view the writers and their novels as representative sites of describable change in a larger historical process. Rather than an innate consciousness or authentic self, it is language as an immense dynamic realm of discursive contact, engagement, struggle, and signifying acts that gives rise to and maintains the subject and her experiences. The act of reading constitutes a major gateway into this discursive realm, and representations of reading in biography and the novels provide a rich opportunity to examine this site of agency.

The aims of this book are to contribute to contemporary theories of agency by situating the practices of reading and writing socially and symbolically; to participate in the recovery of women writers from traditional critical readings which reinscribe subversive authors into the patriarchal paradigm, and to intervene in the discourses of sex and gender in order to create a wider understanding and acceptance of differences among women.

Of the many people who have helped, I want to give particular thanks to Bruce Martin at Drake University, who first introduced me to the vast discursive world of George Eliot. Others to whom I am indebted for friendship and seemingly endless conversations regarding consciousness, reading and writing, discourse, and subjectivity are Sally Barr-Ebest, Wim Coleman, Bernice Hausman, Greg Eiselein and Anne Bartlett. My daughters, Lisa and Marianne Williams, give special meaning to my work, and along the way, their joy and humor have sustained me through some difficult times. A rewarding summer spent as a Visiting Scholar at the Institute for Research on Women at Rutgers University made it possible to begin revising the manuscript, and I want to thank Cora Kaplan for making that summer possible. Avila College has also provided valuable support and release time for which I am most grateful. Above all, I want to express my gratitude to Adelaide Morris and Alan Nagel at the University of Iowa and Esther Labovitz at Pace University for all the questions, resistance, and encouragement.

Introduction:
Women and the Novel

Thus, towards the end of the eighteenth century a change came about which, if I were rewriting history, I should describe more fully and think of greater importance than the Crusades or the Wars of the Roses. The middle-class woman began to write.

The novel alone was young enough to be soft in her hands—another reason, perhaps, why she wrote novels.

Virginia Woolf
A Room of One's Own

For the most part, before Western European women began writing novels, they were forbidden to participate in the public production of their identities and experiences. When a few women did participate, they were often mentored and thus heavily influenced by fathers, husbands and clergy. Using words like the "will of God," "duty," "the demands of motherhood," and "home-queen," the extensive and interconnected discursive formations of religion, science, and the law constituted immense barriers between women and discursive agency.

According to Londa Schiebinger, the democratic movement emerging in Enlightenment thought and in the American and French Revolutions and producing texts like Thomas Paine's *The Rights of Man* and the Declaration of Independence created a new social field, and women's role in this new social field had to be redefined.[1] The challenge was how to deny civil rights to women in the framework of this new era of liberal thought. Subsequently, in order to reinvent and reconsolidate patriarchal power, much of the decisive authority in social and political matters gradually relocated itself from religion to the newly formed discipline of modern medicine. The myths of Eve's fall and women's greater susceptibility to temptation were rewritten as mental and physical feebleness.

Schiebinger argues that the first representations of the female skeleton appearing in European science were not arbitrary, but based on an anatomist's ideal of structure, and they focused attention on politically significant parts of the body.[2] Drawings that portrayed the female skull as smaller than the male skull proved women's intellectual inferiority, and drawings of the larger female pelvis proved women's reproductive purpose. Thomas Laqueur argues that there was not much interest in looking at anatomical and physiological differences between the sexes until these differences became politically important. Rather than being the effects of increased scientific knowledge, new ways of interpreting the body were new ways of representing and constituting social realities.[3]

In the eighteenth and nineteenth centuries, while religious discourse struggled to maintain its power over women, medical discourse reformulated spiritual weakness into a biological vulnerability, locating female bodies in the natural world and marking them as mentally inferior to men. Inequalities coded as "natural" justified social inequalities that were confirmed and authorized by legal and other policy. As late as 1886 in his President's Address to the British Medical Association, Dr. Withers Moore stated that no training could enable women "to do what their sons might have done. Bacon's mother...could not have produced the *Novum Organum*, but she— perhaps she alone—could and did produce Bacon." Moore asked, "Who can exaggerate the importance to the future man of the quality of that mother-stuff?"[4]

In the eighteenth century, at the same time as this shift from religious to medical authority was taking place, Ann Radcliffe received a £500 advance for *The Mysteries of Udolpho*. This was an unprecedented event for a novel, and things began to change. Because of circulating libraries, serial publication and the shilling magazine, novels became available to men and women from various economic backgrounds. For the first time, large numbers of women were participating in literary production and consumption. According to Ian Watt the majority of all eighteenth-century novels came from a female pen, and Elaine Showalter refers to the nineteenth century as the Age of the Female Novelist.[5]

Dale Spender identifies "one hundred good women novelists" before Jane Austen who together wrote almost 600 novels, and she writes that it was women, not men, who made the greater contribution to the novel's development. Significantly, women's education was one of the most frequent themes in these early novels. Referring to the novels written before Austen as "subversive in their own context," Spender writes that they were often and vehemently condemned; that they constituted, to some extent, women's education at the time, and, as a result of reading these novels, women became less passive and more difficult to subordinate.[6] These three aspects—the inordinate fear and condemnation of novels, their educational value, and their effects on women—are central concerns of this book.

Because historical processes position subjects and produce experiences *through discourse*, this book focuses on the historical significance of scenes of reading as critical moments of discursive contact, knowledge production, and agency. In examining their biographies, letters, and novels we see how Brontë, Eliot, and Woolf, although born into sexist and oppressive discourses, acquired the agency to challenge and perform them differently.

Referring to the "reutilizations of identical formulas for contrary objectives," Michel Foucault writes that discourse is a series of discontinuous segments whose tactical function is neither uniform nor stable. Discourse is not subservient to power; rather, power is located within the discourse, and it is necessary to recognize and "make allowance for the complex and unstable process whereby discourse can be both an instrument and an effect of power, but also a hindrance, a stumbling-block, a point of resistance and starting point for an opposing strategy."[7] Due to the potential of discourse to resist, oppose and bring about change, acts of reading and writing take on a decisive importance.

The book's theoretical terms may, at first glance, seem obscure or abstract. Some phrases were borrowed from others writers like "subversive repetition" from Judith Butler and "novelistic discourse" from Mikhail Bakhtin, while other phrases like "scenes of reading" and "discursive agency" were created to suit the book's particular needs. Butler, describing discourses as historically specific organizations of language, writes that they present themselves in the plural, coexist within temporal frames, and institute unpredictable and inadvertent convergence from which discursive possibilities are engendered.[8] A key aspect of this fluid and dynamic discursive process is subversive repetition. A subversive repetition does not merely repeat or imitate traditional attitudes and ideas. Rather, it refuses to conform to or consolidate the status quo. While just similar enough to be culturally intelligible, a subversive repetition disrupts old ways through differences in tone, in recontextualization and location, and in deviant endings. A repetition with a difference displaces the old through ambiguity, irony, hyperbole, parody, and dissonance. As Butler argues, operating within the matrix of power is not the same as replicating uncritically relations of domination. There is the possibility of a repetition of the law that is not its consolidation but its displacement.[9] Although we inherit words with histories, inherit plots and metaphors and although we cannot step outside our historical moment, the accumulation and multiplicity of discourses available—their interanimation, contradictions, and intersections—allow for recombination and redeployment.

Because women are often represented and controlled through discourses regarding the body, one major way to identify subversive repetitions is by close attention to bodily appearance and performance. Bodies, as we can know them, are socially constructed, politically motivated, and subject to change rather than pre-given or natural. The body is a sign and a material practice, permeable and fluid, and continually engaged in encounters and exchanges. The word "body" is often used in the book rather than "subject," "person," or "individual" to evoke more of a sense of the large semiotic space that signifies "woman." The body's "inside" contains interior elements like mind, reason, soul, and heart which together constitute a kind of metaphysical anatomy. The borderline of "inside" and "out" is marked by such aspects as skin color, size, shape, complexion, hair, age, race, and ethnicity which are particularly significant in terms of their historically contingent exchange value. There is also the complex realm of body covering, decoration, and performance. Words like "subject" and "individual" fail to evoke these complex areas of interiority, borderline, covering, decoration and performance. Yet, constructed in discourse, these areas are vital in how and where they position women and in determining how women feel about themselves. Repeating the word "body" and calling attention to bodily details evoke the presence of these areas and the politics of their social construction.

Throughout the book the words "sex" and "gender" are used in the ways that Butler and Foucault define and use the terms. Foucault writes that sexuality is not a stubborn drive, but a historical construct, an especially dense transfer point for relations of power. Sexuality is a set of effects produced in bodies, behaviors, and social relations deriving from a complex political technology, an element in power relations "endowed with the greatest instrumentality: useful for the greatest number of maneuvers and capable of serving as a point of support, as a linchpin, for the most varied strategies." Sexuality gives rise to the notion of sex, and, thus, sex is historically subordinate to sexuality. Foucault argues that we "must not think that by saying yes to sex, one says no to power; on the contrary, one tracks along the course laid out by the general deployment of sexuality."[10] The internal stability and binary frame of sex is secured by casting its duality in a prediscursive domain. However, gender is not to culture as sex is to nature; both sex and gender are culturally constructed, and thus, as Butler argues, the distinction between sex and gender turns out to be no distinction at all.[11]

Throughout the book, in contrast to the word "language," the word "discourse" is used because it illicits more of the socio-political aspects of language. Several such social languages circulate at any particular historical moment, each signaling a particular world view saturated with values, beliefs, and intentions. Novelistic discourse refers to the novel's ability to capture and represent such a swarm of social languages in all its diversity, presenting simultaneous and radically different figurations as the author of a heteroglot text acknowledges a multiplicity of truths and the dialogue resulting from their mutual presence. Novelistic discourse is able to re-present the dialogue of historical and social voices in the voices of narrator, characters, and inserted genres. While reading novelistic discourse, women can still feel the pressures to conform, but can also hear the slips and contradictions among truths. Such "hearing" can lead to an understanding of truth and knowledge not as a particular set of beliefs but as an ongoing struggle over interpretation. Women can seize this opportunity to dis-identify with certain oppressive ideologies and reconstruct other roles and relationships.

In their development as readers and writers, Brontë, Eliot, and Woolf confronted a set of coexistent and interlocking representations of women circulating in religious, legal, and scientific discourse. These patriarchal constructions of women do not involve all priests, lawyers, and doctors, but are widespread and powerful discourses spoken by some. This attitude toward women, politically motivated and explicitly stated in classical, philosophical, and religious texts, is inherited by each generation as part of religious training and a classical education.

As late as 1881, Dr. Matthews Duncan, president of the Edinburgh Obstetrical Society, defended the value of medical students studying Greek and Latin, stating that "through them pass the roots of our language, our philosophy, our arts, our sciences."[12] The pervasive recommendation to study and revere classical texts illustrates how these texts sustain attitudes about women from one generation to the next, from teacher to pupil, and even from one country to another. The power of this androcentric and sometimes misogynist point of view is out of all proportion to the number of its proponents, and the power is characteristic of the discourse more than of any individual who speaks it. Viewing the female body as inferior, reproductive and ornamental in purpose, these patriarchal constructions justify a belief in male supremacy and subsequent relations of power and control. Examples of religious, legal and medical discourse appear throughout this book in order to reveal the dominant historical attitudes toward women previous to and prevalent during the lives of Brontë, Eliot, and Woolf. These examples provide a historical context within which to evaluate the subversive repetitions enacted in their novels.

In describing the process of discursive agency through an examination of biography and literature, a considerable amount of attention seems to be give to the individual. However, the view of discourse and agency framing this discussion actually places less emphasis on the individual than the subject/object dichotomy of the Western philosophical tradition, the subject-predicate relation of syntax and grammar, or the preference for the active over the passive voice indicates or allows. In this discussion "individual" refers to a nexus of discursive contacts, intersection, and hybridization resulting from immersion in scenes of reading and writing.

Both Mary Poovey and Butler help conceptualize this anti-individualist perspective toward discourse and agency. Rather than origins, Poovey also investigates the dynamics and interrelations of signifying acts with other signifying acts. Noting that the ego-centered subject is a historical construct, she writes: "no individual can originate meaning nor can he or she contain or foresee the effects the text will produce."[13] Toward the end of *Gender Trouble,* Butler comments on her use of the word "I," writing that "it is the grammar itself that deploys and enables this 'I,' even as the 'I' that insists itself here repeats, redeploys, and...contests the philosophical grammar by which it is both enabled and restricted."[14] While my point is that certain readers and writers are more active elements in this process, still I choose the phrase "discursive agency" as a process that allows for change over and above a discursive agent necessary to the change.

We can know past authors only through discourses—the discourses of autobiography, letters, diaries and biography. The author does not function as an emerging self but as a historical and social nexus through which discourses intersected, argued with and transformed one another. In her discussion of identity, Butler abandons an epistemological account where identity is fixed and where self-knowledge implies both self-discovery and insight. Instead, she shifts to one that locates identity formation in discourse as an effect of signifying practices. The question becomes not how am "I" expressing myself, but how am "I" performing a process of rule-bound discourses. To enter into the repetitive practices of signification—to perform— is not a choice; agency is located in the possibility of a variation and displacement of the repetition. From this perspective, the author operates as a site of discursive experiences, as a channel through which multiple and diverse discourses flow and intermingle and are subsequently infused into the literature.

It seems pointless to discuss a reality outside of discursive practices, when ultimately, whether it be a natural disaster or a work of art, any attempt to describe, understand or share that reality takes place in and through language. In discussing how difference is relationally constituted, Joan Scott writes that we need to attend to the "historical processes that, through discourse, position subjects and produce their experiences. It is not individuals who have experience, but subjects who are constituted through experience." Experience, then, is what we seek to explain; that about which knowledge is produced.[15] Scott is not discussing a new form of linguistic determinism; rather, she is refusing to separate experience and language, and, like Foucault and Butler, insisting on the productive quality of discourse. Although subjects are constituted discursively, Scott notes that "there are conflicts among discursive systems, contradictions within any one of them, multiple meanings possible for the concepts they deploy."[16]

This book argues that an awareness of these conflicts, contradictions, multiple meanings, and subsequent creative possibilities comes through scenes of reading.

Numerous scenes of reading occur in the novels discussed. For example, in the novel's first pages Jane Eyre notes reading Goldsmith's *History of Rome* and drawing parallels between the emperors and John Reed. In *The Voyage Out* Rachel Vinrace, in the midst of pressures to marry, reads the *Works of Henrik Ibsen* and acts out the parts in Ibsen's plays for days. On the first pages of *The Mill on the Floss,* Maggie Tulliver sits with Defoe's *The History of the Devil* on her knees while in the same room her father and Mr. Riley discuss her brother Tom's formal education. Defoe's text is open to a picture of swimming a witch, where a woman accused of witchcraft will float if she is guilty and drown if she is innocent. Maggie's complex scene of reading is a site inhabited by tension and contradiction where the reader is both in the text and in her context. It is a site where Maggie encounters Defoe's disrespect for authority while wondering what good drowning would do an innocent woman and overhearing the sexism spoken by her father and Mr. Riley. These scenes, whether in a father's library, the British Museum, or a room of one's own, constitute sites of agency where one contacts the power and knowledge of discourse and can enter the struggle over representation and meaning.

Fluent in seven languages and one of the nineteenth century's most learned scholars, George Eliot serves as a model of the woman reader, and so, the book begins with her. Chapter One provides an overview of her reading, focusing on her German translations and subsequent association with Karl Marx. The exploration demonstrates in detail the complex dynamics of reading as a creative process of contact, discernment, recombination and development. Chapter Two demonstrates how Eliot's reading experiences repeat themselves in the character of Maggie Tulliver in *The Mill on the Floss.* Precocious, witchy and passionate, Maggie is a voracious reader, and this chapter analyzes the novel's witch motif and three of the numerous books she reads, Defoe's *The History of the Devil,* Thomas à Kempis's *The Imitation of Christ,* and Madame de Staël's *Corinne, or Italy.*

Chapter Three begins by discussing early scenes of reading and writing in the life of Charlotte Brontë, scenes which enabled her to write narratives radically different from other literature of the time.

Brontë repeats these scenes in *Jane Eyre*, giving Jane the power to refuse harmful and degrading perceptions of her body, to travel to other places, and to gain symbolic power. Chapter Four analyzes the politics of location emerging at the intersection of Brontë's physical, social, and geographical marginalization and her reading and writing that repeats itself in the character of Lucy Snowe in *Villette*. In reading *Villette* as a critique and rejection of the center as oppressive and exploitive for women, in reading Lucy's continual displacement as a study in the politics of location, I read against an attitude toward "home" prevalent in much narrative before and after Brontë, and I read against an abundance of criticism that discusses Lucy in terms of morbidity, deprivation, and defeat.

Chapter Five turns to Virginia Woolf who, even though she was denied a formal education, read widely in the classics, literature, and history. Her personal experiences with incest, breakdown and the rest cure in combination with her extensive reading resulted in a radically different point of view. This chapter examines the site of intersection where nineteenth-century medical discourse, Woolf's family, and her father's library collide.

Chapter Six examines the unfolding of Woolf's radical point of view in her first novel *The Voyage Out*. The heroine, Rachel Vinrace, discovers the agency in reading at the same time that the novel performs a detailed analysis of the institution of marriage. Chapter Seven reviews the issues of sexuality, dress, the law, romantic love, and scenes of reading and writing in the context of the fantastic *Orlando,* which moves through five centuries and deliberately marks the protagonist's sex change midway in the text. Mocking the essential and natural body, in *Orlando* Woolf demonstrates that the body is not a "being," but a variable boundary, a surface whose permeability is politically regulated and subject to change.

Discursive agency results from contacting and hearing disturbances and contradictions in various belief systems, from the possibility of confronting and analyzing contrasting points of view. Knowledge becomes an ongoing enterprise sometimes caught in fear and subject to relations of power. The reader begins to understand knowledge not as a set of truths to be memorized but as a dynamic and ongoing struggle, a process that can define and construct experience through representation. Finally, the reader begins to realize the power of participating in this discursive arena as a writer of texts.

Still, acquiring agency through discourse is not easy. Woolf's life, marked by bouts of mental illness and suicide by drowning, speaks the difficulty of managing female giftedness in the midst of an androcentric world. Yet, and this is the important point, a change took place between the sixteenth-century world of Shakespeare's sister Judith and Woolf's writing, and the novel in the hands of women played a major role in this change. Beginning with extensive reading experiences, women came to challenge and refuse reductive views and construct other narratives and other choices, spotlighting the rich diversity among women as well as their energy, intelligence and desires.

The German Connection in George Eliot

Most of us who turn to any subject we love remember some morning or evening hour when we got on a high stool to reach down an untried volume, or sat with parted lips listening to a new talker, or for very lack of books began to listen to the voices within, as the first traceable beginning of our love.

George Eliot
Middlemarch

Nathless I love words; they are the quoits, the bows, the staves that furnish the gymnasium of the mind. Without them in our present condition, our intellectual strength would have no implementation.

George Eliot
Letters, September 1841

As a young girl and woman, George Eliot worked actively to educate herself, writing countless letters expressing her reactions and responses to the books she read. The nine volumes of *The George Eliot Letters* constitute a record of her engagement with the important writers, books, and ideas in circulation from 1836 to 1880. At the age of five she went to boarding school, and at the age of seven she began reading Walter Scott's *Waverley*. Her teacher Maria Lewis took a special interest in her, recognizing her genius and providing encouragement and support. Having mastered everything at the first school at thirteen, Eliot was sent to another. There she studied music, drawing, English, French, history and mathematics and read Shakespeare, Milton, Bunyan, Pope, Young, Cowper, Southey and Byron.

When Eliot returned home at sixteen to care for her father, she continued her omnivorous reading and studying. The squire of Chilvers Coton lent her books and Mrs. Charles Newdegate invited her to borrow freely from the Arbury Hall library. Her father, proud of her reputation as a scholar, allowed her to buy the books she wanted and arranged for Italian and German lessons each week. Gordon Haight writes that soon she was reading Botta's *Storia d'Italia,* Silvio Pellico's *Le mie Prigioni,* and Schiller's *Wallenstein.*[1] At the age of twenty she wrote:

> We cannot, at least those who ever read to any purpose at all, we cannot I say help being modified by the ideas that pass through our minds. We hardly wish to lay claim to such elasticity as retains no impress. We are active beings too.... [H]ence our actions have their share in the effects of our reading....[2]

In this passage Eliot displays her express understanding of the power of discourse to modify ideas and alter experience. Later, in examining the German translation of *Middlemarch,* she displayed her sensitivity to the difference one word can make, writing, "I have my own fastidious choice of words which seem to me the very flesh & blood of my thoughts, & I naturally find the substitution of other words a sort of flaying process followed by the application of the plaisters to serve instead of skin."[3] Referring to words as the very flesh and blood of thoughts and associating textual disfigurement with the disfigurement of the body, Eliot reveals a deep sense of the materiality of language and her intimacy with it.

References and allusions to other writers such as Shakespeare, Walter Scott and Wordsworth abound in Eliot's letters and echo throughout her fiction, and she is frequently discussed in terms of their influence. There are well over one hundred references to Shakespeare in *The George Eliot Letters,* for example, and she wrote about Scott, "my worship for Scott is peculiar. I began to read him when I was seven years old, and afterwards when I was grown up and living alone with my Father.... No other writer would serve as a substitute for Scott, and my life at that time would have been much more difficult without him" (5:175). In 1839 after reading three volumes of *The Poetical Works of William Wordsworth,* she wrote, "I never before met with so many of my own feelings," and again in

1877 she expressed her love for the "incomparable Wordsworth" (1:34, 6:439).

Haight states that with "sure instinct for the significant" Eliot turned to Spinoza around 1843, whose *Tractatus Theologico-politicus* was the "true source of all the Higher Criticism" (1:xliv). In the 1840s she translated the *Tractatus Theologico-politicus* from the medieval Latin, and in the 1850s she translated Spinoza's *Ethics*. Thomas Deegan refers to the Spinoza-like phrases and ideas which begin to appear in her letters, and Elizabeth Ermarth, in discussing the effects of Spinoza on Eliot's moral vision, notes his tolerance and inclusiveness, the importance he placed on knowledge in achieving freedom, and his belief in the creative power of individuals.[4] In addition to Spinoza, Shakespeare, Scott and Wordsworth, any discussion of influence on Eliot should also include the Bible, Milton, Comte, Charlotte Brontë, George Sand, Spencer, Darwin, Tennyson, Dickens, Strauss and Feuerbach. No doubt, there are others, and there is always the possibility of attributing too much significance to any one influence, especially when Eliot's remarks regarding an individual writer are taken out of context and given undue weight.

This chapter examines the importance of Eliot's reading and translating of German higher criticism, especially that of David Strauss and Ludwig Feuerbach, and her subsequent relationship with Karl Marx, connections often overlooked or dealt with hastily in discussions of her work. At the same time, it is necessary to keep in mind that no one influence dominated her thought. Eliot herself stated as much in a letter to Sara Sophia Hennell in 1849, explaining how reading helped her to make "new combinations":

> I wish you thoroughly to understand that the writers who have most profoundly influenced me...are not in the least oracles to me. It is just possible that I may not embrace one of their opinions, that I may wish my life to be shaped quite differently from theirs. For instance it would signify nothing to me if a very wise person were to stun me with proofs that Rousseau's views...are miserably erroneous.... I might admit all this—and it would be not the less true that Rousseau's genius has sent that electric thrill through my intellectual and moral frame which has awakened me to new perceptions. It is simply that the rushing mighty wind of his inspiration...the fire of his genius has so fused together old thoughts and prejudices that I have been ready to make new combinations. (1:277–78)

Distancing herself from any particular writer, Eliot understood the possibility to reshape and recombine past and present discourses. Blending narration and dialogue with poetic description, philosophy, and irony, the medium of her intellect transformed diverse systems of thought into novelistic discourse.

Eliot did considerable amounts of reading in German higher criticism and philosophy, translating Strauss's *Life of Jesus, Critically Examined* in 1844–46 and Feuerbach's *The Essence of Christianity* in 1853–54. In 1854 she left with George Henry Lewes for an eight-month stay in Germany to work on his life of Goethe. Haight, noting that Eliot translated most of the long prose passages and read the whole manuscript with care, writes that this important biography "might be considered a composite production."[5] William Baker's annotated catalogue represents roughly 60% of Eliot and Lewes's books at the time of Eliot's death, and around 25% of this portion of their books or 600 volumes were in German. Baker writes that the books illustrate their "preference for and immersion in Continental and especially German thought."[6] These various experiences in reading, translating, research, and traveling positioned Eliot in the mainstream of German intellectual activity.

In 1835 Strauss published his *Life of Jesus, Critically Examined,* one of the most important publications of the century. Horton Harris writes that "theology was split in two by the publication of the *Life of Jesus* and...the year 1835 was the most important theological milestone of the century.... Strauss became a notorious celebrity overnight, and was everywhere regarded as the arch-fiend of the true Christian faith."[7] A detailed inquiry into the historicity of the Gospels, *The Life of Jesus* gave shape to the discipline of biblical criticism, according to Marilyn Massey, and through its influence on the Hegelians and Marx, it altered the course of European and world history.[8] Called immoral and heretical, Strauss's work revealed inconsistencies and contradictions and was seen as a serious threat to the existing political order. Conservatives thought that such biblical criticism prepared the way for political criticism, and they opposed a principle that allowed every objection against a system to be printed and made public. This theological quarrel over the relation of human reason to the Gospels was also a political quarrel over freedom of expression and freedom of the press.[9]

Disproving the historicity of the evangelical narratives was not new; Strauss's real contribution was his theory that events and acts recorded in the Gospels were meant to glorify Jesus and were deduced from the Old Testament, thus fulfilling the Old Testament prediction and descriptions of a Messiah. Strauss argued that what had appeared to be historical truth, was, in fact, a product of human consciousness. In myth, the source of inspiration was not immediate divine agency, but the spirit of a people or community, and, thus, the Christ of the gospels was a product of that particular historical period.

Understanding this change in focus from Jesus to the community can free readers from submission to a past exalted individual and past consciousness to a recognition of the collective human potential for agency in the present. Massey comments, "The Young Germans, and many of the left-wing Hegelians, including Marx, had sought literary forms to express visions of a democratic society and to effect change. *The Life of Jesus* gave them such a form in theology."[10] Belief in the orthodox Christ and support for the hereditary monarchy were held to be intertwined. The threatening nature of Strauss's text issued from his belief that the common people rather than the exalted individual leader create meaning and interpret history. In this radical democracy, humanity takes the place of Christ; the true Christ is the human species.

Strauss's disbelief concerning Christ's divinity had been thoroughly anticipated by Eliot's reading of Charles Hennell's *Inquiry Concerning the Origins of Christianity* and made little further change in her views. However, because of Strauss's shift from the individual to the group, his influence emerges in Eliot's fiction in the problematic nature of hereditary wealth and power as seen in the Donnithornes in *Adam Bede,* for example, the Cass family in *Silas Marner,* Mr. Brooke in *Middlemarch,* and Grandcourt in *Daniel Deronda.* Rather than the aristocrats, middle to lower class characters like Adam Bede and Felix Holt and marginalized characters like Ladislaw and Daniel Deronda grow and develop through the narratives to assume positions of power in the end. In 1868 a writer for the *Daily News* argued that compared to Eliot, "No one in our day has given more adequate expression to the sentiments of persons who, though born in a lowly station and playing their part therein with cheerfulness and success, are yet endowed with the qualities which suffice for occupying more prominent places on the world stage."[11] In addition, the notion that "Jesus" was a product of a historical community—both those Old Testament writers who predicted his coming and the disciples who fulfilled the prediction—reveals the connectedness of individuals, the human web, in creating history and culture. Herein lies one source of Eliot's emphasis on sympathy, duty, and community. Actions, no matter how insignificant they appear, affect others and shape the future. In 1853 she wrote, "I begin to feel for other people's wants and sorrows a little more than I used to do. Heaven help us! said the old religions; the new one, from its very lack of that faith, will teach us all the more to help one another" (2:82). In Eliot's narrative world, acquiring a social consciousness which includes understanding and appreciation of others becomes one of the most important aspects of human development.

Like Strauss's *Life of Jesus,* Feuerbach's work *The Essence of Christianity* was viewed as subversive, heretical, and dangerous. The author was condemned by the majority of his contemporaries, and the work's "inopportuneness had the effect, if not of sending his own skin off to market, at least of sacrificing his academic 'career' immediately and irrevocably."[12] In the Preface he wrote, "Briefly, the 'Idea' is to me only faith in the historical future...it has for me only a political and moral significance;...I attach myself, in direct opposition to the Hegelian philosophy, only to *realism,* to materialism..." [original emphasis].[13] In contrast to Strauss's idealistic view of the collective spirit, Feuerbach was a materialist, and this materialism constitutes a profound difference between the two.

Feuerbach expressed the need to transfer the emphasis from some external Sovereign Being to human beings and their social interaction. Rather than emphasizing the spirit, he constructed humans as "species-beings," that is social beings: "Only where man has contact and friction with his fellow-man are wit and sagacity kindled; hence there is more wit in the town than in the country, more in great towns than in small ones. Only where man suns and warms himself in the proximity of man arise feeling and imagination."[14] This attitude toward the country is, obviously, not Romantic, but it is an attitude shared by Marx and Engels who more caustically refer to the "idiocy of rural life."[15] It is also an attitude Eliot expresses in *Middlemarch.*

In the novel when Mr. Brooke visits Mr. Dagley, the tenant farmer at Freeman's End, the narrator pauses to comment on Dagley's poverty. In this passage, which merits quoting at length, Eliot translates Feuerbach's attitude toward the country into novelistic discourse:

> It is true that an observer, under that softening influence of the fine arts which makes other people's hardships picturesque, might have been delighted with this homestead called Freeman's End: the old house had dormer-windows in the dark-red roof, two of the chimneys were choked with ivy...the mouldering garden wall with hollyhocks peeping over it was a perfect study of highly-mingled subdued colour.... [T]he pauper labourers...the scanty dairy of cows...the very pigs and white ducks seeming to wander about the uneven neglected yard as if in low spirits from feeding on a too meagre quality of rinsings—all these objects under the quiet light of a sky marbled with high clouds would have made a sort of picture which we have all paused over as a "charming bit,".... Mr. Dagley himself made a figure in the landscape, carrying a pitch-fork and wearing his milking-hat....
>
> Some who follow the narrative of his experience may wonder at the midnight darkness of Mr Dagley; but nothing was easier in those times than for an hereditary farmer of his grade to be ignorant, in spite somehow of having a rector in the twin parish who was a gentleman to the backbone,...a landlord who had gone into everything, especially fine art and social improvement, and all the lights of Middlemarch only three miles off.... Poor Dagley read a few verses sometimes on a Sunday evening, and the world was at least not darker to him than it had been before. Some things he knew thoroughly, namely, the slovenly habits of farming, and the awkwardness of weather, stock and crops, at Freeman's End—so called apparently by way of sarcasm, to imply that a man was free to quit it if he chose, but that there was no earthly "beyond" open to him.[16]

Disrupting the Romantic trope of the beauty and contentment of simple people in rural settings, in this passage Eliot uses irony to criticize a tendency to make poverty and hardship picturesque, and she points out class injustices and the pathetic misfortune of being illiterate. This realistic treatment of poverty and exploitation in conjunction with Eliot's German translations strongly suggests a relationship with Karl Marx.

Eliot was born in 1819 and died in 1880; Marx was born in 1818 and died in 1883. In August of 1849 Marx sailed for London and lived there for the remainder of his life. In 1851 Eliot also made London her permanent home. During most of 1851 and 1852 Eliot lived at

142 Strand, the home and literary headquarters of John Chapman, editor of the *Westminster Review,* and in 1852 she became assistant editor of the journal. Scientists like T. H. Huxley and Richard Owen and political refugees like Mazzini and Ferdinand Freiligrath gravitated to 142 Strand, which was, according to Haight, London's "centre of enlightened radicalism."[17] Finally, Eliot and Marx are buried near one another in Highgate Cemetery. Such coincidence would be no great matter if it went no further, but the physical proximity symbolizes a more profound intellectual link.

From 1836–1838 Marx studied philosophy, law, history, English, and Italian at the University of Berlin. As one of the young Hegelian radicals, he read and praised Feuerbach, and in 1845 Marx wrote his "Theses on Feuerbach." When Engels published the "Theses" in 1888, he referred to it as "the brilliant germ of the new world outlook" (143). It is this "new world outlook," this materialism, immediately seized upon by Eliot and Marx that makes a comparison of the two significant, for both writers extracted from their reading of Feuerbach major premises regarding God and religion, identity, and social relations that would influence their later thinking.

Significantly, both Eliot and Marx referred to religion as the opiate of the people. In religion people can limit themselves to self-consciousness and self-discovery, devoted primarily to the goal of personal salvation. The value of earthly suffering is commonplace in religious rhetoric; that is, material deprivation enhances spiritual intensity. Feuerbach wrote that "the most genuine Christians have declared that earthly good draws man away from God, whereas adversity, suffering, afflictions lead him back to God, and hence alone are suited to Christians"; the "more limited a man's sphere of vision, the less he knows of history, Nature, philosophy—the more ardently does he cling to his religion"; "Faith is the opposite of love.... It was faith, not love, not reason, which invented Hell"; "*In faith there lies a malignant principle*" [original emphasis]; and "Faith necessarily passes into hatred, hatred into persecution."[18] These particular statements display the intensity of Feuerbach's attack on Christianity. The English words are Eliot's, of course, carefully chosen during translation, and in 1854 she stated: "With the ideas of Feuerbach I everywhere agree" (2:153).

In 1843 in his "Contribution to the Critique of Hegel's *Philosophy of Right:* Introduction," Marx stated: "Religion is the sigh of the oppressed creature, the sentiment of a heartless world, and the soul of soulless conditions. It is the *opium* of the people" [original emphasis] (54). In 1860 in a letter to her close friend the feminist activist Barbara Leigh Smith Bodichon, Eliot wrote:

> I have faith in the working-out of higher possibilities than the Catholic or any other church has presented, and those who have strength to wait and endure, are bound to accept no formula which their whole souls—their intellect as well as their emotions—do not embrace with entire reverence. The highest "calling and election" is to *do without opium* and live through all our pain with conscious, clear-eyed endurance [original emphasis]. (3:366)

Both Marx and Eliot used and emphasized the word "opium" in describing the effects of religion, underscoring religion's thoughtless attraction and seduction and the nature of their objection. The negative consequences of religion vary from self-absorption and alienation to the justification of oppression and persecution of others.

Eliot foregrounds this theory of religion in *The Mill on the Floss* in the concluding chapter of Book Four where the text marks Maggie Tulliver as thirteen. At this point Bob Jakins brings her Thomas à Kempis's *The Imitation of Christ,* and only nine pages later, the text marks Maggie as seventeen. In these nine pages, pages that mark the passing of four years in a book that lasts for a total of eleven years, the narrator moves quickly from the specifics of Maggie's static relationship with Thomas à Kempis to speak generally about the connection between religion, attending church services, and class structure. The *Mill*'s narrator contends that in

> writing the history of unfashionable families one is apt to fall into a tone of emphasis which is very far from being the tone of good society where...no subjects being eligible but such as can be touched with a light and graceful irony. But then, good society has its claret and its velvet-carpets, its dinner-engagements six weeks deep, its opera and its faëry ball-rooms; rides off its ennui on thoroughbred horses, lounges at the club, has to keep clear of crinoline vortices, gets its science done by Faraday, and its religion by the superior clergy who are to be met in the best houses: how should it have time or need for belief and emphasis? But good society, floated on gossamer wings of light irony, is of very expensive production; requiring nothing less than a wide and arduous national life condensed in deafening factories, cramping

itself in mines, sweating at furnaces, grinding, hammering, weaving under
more or less oppression of carbonic acid.... This wide national life is based
entirely on emphasis—the emphasis of want.... Under such circumstances,
there are many among its myriads of souls who have absolutely needed an
emphatic belief.... Some have an emphatic belief in alcohol...but the rest
require something that good society calls "enthusiasm," something that will
present motives in an entire absence of high prizes....[19]

This social critique, this point of view toward wealth and religion, is
one of several places in *The Mill* where Marx and Eliot's philosophies
intersect. The class structure described consists of a few fashionable
families living off the labor of the majority; the expensive
reproduction of good society—the velvet carpets and thoroughbred
horses—requires the exploitation of workers and their families. This
relation between good society and poverty requires religious
enthusiasm to reproduce itself—requires that selfless and resigned
state of mind that looks to life after death as the reward for earthly
suffering. Attending church and enthusiastically espousing it as the
right and decent thing to do serves the economic interests of the
middle and upper classes. Only in the institutionalized space of the
Church do the two classes meet: the workers to take their opium and
the bourgeoisie to valorize the taking. What the narrator calls
religious "enthusiasm" is the price tag of "good society," a society
that by definition requires hunger, ignorance, and sickness for great
numbers of the population.

In addition to the narrator's commentary, the relations of
production between capitalist and worker emerge at the level of plot
and character between Mr. Tulliver and Mr. Wakem. The lawyer Mr.
Wakem is in the upper circles of St. Ogg's society, and he knows "the
stepping-stones that would carry him through very muddy bits of
practice." Wakem is a man "who had made a large fortune, had a
handsome house among the trees at Tofton, and decidedly the finest
stock of port-wine in the neighbourhood." When he attends church,
he sits under "the handsomest of mural monuments erected to the
memory of his wife." After Tulliver's bankruptcy, the narrator
ironically explores Wakem's motivation in buying the mill: "He had
once had the pleasure of putting an old enemy of his into one of the
St Ogg's alms-houses, to the rebuilding of which he had given a large
subscription; and here was an opportunity of providing for another by

making him his own servant."[20] Once Maggie's father loses the mill and works for a wage, an exploitive relation develops between him and Wakem, and it is this change—"the unhappy-looking father...the childish, bewildered mother; the little sordid tasks that filled the hours"—that directly causes Maggie to embrace Thomas à Kempis.

Thus, Eliot demonstrates in *The Mill* how poverty leads to depression and despair, which, in turn, can lead one to take up a position of religious renunciation and self-abasement. Feuerbach explains: "Pleasure, joy, expands man; trouble, suffering, contracts and concentrates him; in suffering man denies the reality of the world;...he is absorbed in himself, in his own soul. The soul thus self-absorbed, self-concentrated, seeking satisfaction in itself alone, denying the world, idealistic in relation to the world...—this soul is God."[21] Feuerbach hoped to change heavenly citizens into world citizens, believers into thinkers, and theologians into anthropologists, and it is difficult to imagine two philosophies as contradistinct as those of Thomas à Kempis and Feuerbach.

As well as their common Feuerbachian inheritance, Eliot and Marx moved beyond Feuerbach's materialist humanism in similar ways to develop and share two additional ideas. Both Eliot and Marx stressed the danger of conceptualizing people in terms of self-consciousness, the individual ego, or the (innate) self, and again we see the influence of Strauss. In his polemic against the ego, "On the Jewish Question" (1843), Marx stated:

> Human emancipation will only be complete when the real, individual man has absorbed into himself the abstract citizen; when as an individual man, in his everyday life, in his work, and in his relationships, he has become a *species-being*; and when he has recognized and organized his own powers...as *social* powers so that he no longer separates this social power from himself as *political* power [original emphasis]. (46)

Several of Eliot's characters like Adam Bede, Dorothea, Ladislaw, Romola, Felix Holt, and Daniel Deronda enact this movement from "self" to social being with varying degrees of success. The agency Eliot and Marx assign to language in constructing and reconstructing conventions of personality and experience was quite forward-looking, and in this attitude toward language and "self," they had little in common with the traditional Victorian attempt to uncover and develop the buried self. In terms of both religion and egotism, Marx and Eliot asked that people look outside their personal dreams and desires, to historical, political, and social relations as cause and cure for pressing social problems.

Both Eliot and Marx embraced a materialist point of view. In the *Manifesto of the Communist Party* (1848), Marx and Engels tersely asked, "Does it require deep intuition to comprehend that man's ideas, views, and conceptions, in one word, man's consciousness, changes with every change in the conditions of his material existence, in his social relations and in his social life?" (489). In "The Natural History of German Life" (1856), Eliot stated that the "selfish instincts are not subdued by the sight of buttercups, nor is integrity in the least established by that classic rural occupation, sheep-washing. To make men moral, something more is requisite than to turn them out to grass"; and "there is an analogous relation between the moral tendencies of men and the social conditions they have inherited."[22] These quotations do not identify an internal or transcendent spirit expressing itself through the world; rather, that spirit is constructed by social and material conditions. Morality results from a just and decent socio-economic climate in which people can grow to goodness.

In her essay on William Lecky's *The Influence of Rationalism* (1865), Eliot focused on the ability to recognize these significant changes in material existence and thus consciousness. She defined "external Reason" as a material force determined by physical science and causing the rejection of the miraculous. This "cultivated Reason," this rationalism is

the sum of conditions resulting from the laws of material growth, from changes produced by great historical collisions shattering the structures of ages and making new highways for events and ideas.... No undiscovered laws accounting for small phenomena going forward under drawing-room tables are likely to affect the tremendous facts of the increase of population, the rejection of convicts by our colonies, the exhaustion of the soil by cotton plantations, which urge even upon the foolish certain questions, certain claims, certain views concerning the scheme of the world, that can never again be silenced. No séances at a guinea a head for the sake of being pinched by "Mary Jane" can annihilate railways, steamships, and electric telegraphs, which are demonstrating the interdependence of all human interests....[23]

Human consciousness is a consequence of specific historical conditions, and progress issues from the transformation of a historically produced self-consciousness to a historically produced social consciousness. Improved conditions result from an alteration in material existence, not from prayer, suffering, or sacrifice.

Marx and Engels summarized the upheaval in German thought—"the putrescence of the absolute spirit"—in "The German Ideology" (1845–46):

> The decomposition of the Hegelian philosophy, which began with Strauss, has developed into a universal ferment into which all the "powers of the past" are swept.... Principles ousted one another, heroes of the mind overthrew each other with unheard-of rapidity, and in the three years 1842–45 more of the past was swept away in Germany than at other times in three centuries....
>
> When the last spark of its life had failed, the various components of this *caput mortuum* began to decompose, entered into *new combinations* and formed new substances [emphasis added]. (147)[24]

In the letter to Sara Sophia Hennell cited earlier, Eliot also referred to the possibility of "new combinations," and her personal movement from Evangelical Calvinism to radical skepticism paralleled the general upheaval Marx and Engels outlined here. Her translations of Strauss and Feuerbach, her association with the *Westminster Review* and first years in London, and her decision to live with a married man constituted radical acts. Yet, she experienced compelling but contradictory needs—to earn money, to participate in the literary practices and traditions of her time, and to speak her mind. Novelistic discourse, irony, and a male pseudonym were the vehicles through which she could negotiate her financial needs, philosophy, style of living, and ambition.

In describing Eliot's first years in London, A. S. Byatt writes that it was an "immense increase of freedom and life. She mixed with others of her own kind—the Insurgents; like herself, they were not part of the established social and religious hierarchy, but were liberal, questioning, free-thinking, interested in reform."[25] Eliot went on to achieve great fame during her life, and in 1880 after her death, Herbert Spencer and others sent telegrams and collected signatures to urge the Dean to admit her to Westminster Abbey. Spencer wrote T.

H. Huxley for his support, and Huxley's response reveals an attitude then current toward Eliot's life and work:

> MY DEAR SPENCER—Your telegram which reached me on Friday evening caused me great perplexity....
>
> Westminster Abbey is a Christian Church and not a Pantheon, and the Dean thereof is officially a Christian priest, and we ask him to bestow exceptional Christian honours by this burial in the Abbey. George Eliot is known not only as a great writer, but as a person whose life and opinions were in notorious antagonism to Christian practice in regard to marriage, and Christian theory in regard to dogma. How am I to tell the Dean that I think he ought to read over the body of a person who did not repent of what the Church considers mortal sin, a service not one solitary proposition in which she would have accepted for truth while she was alive?
>
> You tell me that Mrs. Cross wished for the funeral in the Abbey. While I desire to entertain the greatest respect for her wishes, I am very sorry to hear it.... One cannot eat one's cake and have it too. Those who elect to be free in thought and deed must not hanker after the rewards, if they are to be so called, which the world offers to those who put up with its fetters.
>
> Thus, however I look at the proposal it seems to me to be a profound mistake, and I can have nothing to do with it.[26]

One could say that Huxley's tone and attitude and Eliot's exclusion from Westminster mark the extent of her radical life and views. Yet, the writer of *The Daily News* article quoted earlier called the "Address to Working Men, By Felix Holt" a "Tory manifesto" and *Blackwood's Magazine* a magazine "which has steadfastly adhered to the fortunes of the recognised leaders of the Tory party."[27] For whom and in what ways, then, was Eliot a radical?

For the purposes of this discussion, I have described Eliot and Marx as Feuerbachian siblings, highlighting their common reading experiences in German higher criticism in order to spotlight shared ideas sometimes neglected in critical approaches to Eliot's fiction. Still, there are important differences as well. As early as 1856, through her review of Riehl in "The Natural History of German Life," Eliot argued for social policy founded on the study of people as they are, on "the Natural History of social bodies"—rather than on abstract democratic and socialistic theories. The study of a fragment of society, the small group of Parisian *proletaire* or English factory-workers, cannot be the basis for a universal social policy except on paper and "can never be carried into successful practice. The conditions of German society are altogether different from those of French, of English, or of Italian society."[28] Also, later in her life, Eliot does not seem to be the same kind of radical Hale White described in 1885 when he wrote to the *Athenaeum* "to correct an impression which Mr. Cross's book may possibly produce." White, who lived in Chapman's house while Eliot lived there, wrote:

> To put it very briefly, I think he [Cross] has made her too "respectable." She was really one of the most sceptical, unusual creatures I ever knew, and it was this side of her character which to me was the most attractive....
>
>   I can see her now, with her hair over her shoulders, the easy chair half sideways to the fire, her feet over the arms, and a proof in her hands, in that dark room at the back of No. 142, and I confess I hardly recognize her in the pages of Mr. Cross's—on many accounts—most interesting volumes. I do hope that in some future edition, or in some future work, the salt and spice will be restored to the records of George Eliot's entirely unconventional life. As the matter now stands she has not had full justice done to her, and she has been removed from the class—the great and noble church, if I may so call it of the Insurgents, to one more genteel, but certainly not so interesting.[29]

If the later Eliot were significantly different from this image of a young radical, ironically, the completion of *Felix Holt, The Radical* in 1866 may have heralded the change. This change may have been caused by a complex set of factors, including, perhaps, Eliot's special sense of her audience, pressures from her editor John Blackwood, social ostracism, financial success and fame, and "marriage" to Lewes and the mothering of his sons. Two texts in particular capture the differences between Marx and Eliot, the "Manifesto of the Communist Party" and the "Address to Working Men, By Felix Holt."

The Manifesto, commissioned by the Communist League, was published in English in 1850 in the *Red Republican*. At Blackwood's request, just after the second Reform Bill in 1867, Eliot wrote the "Address to Working Men," published as the opening article in *Maga* in 1868. Although eighteen years separate these texts, they seem to respond directly to one another, thus reflecting the dominant sides in the debate. Both texts identify and discuss the masses, class struggle, the unions, and the importance of history; however, they differ in terms of their ideas regarding effects and solutions.

Whereas Marx and Engels state that the "ruling ideas of each age have ever been the ideas of its ruling class" and "Communism abolished eternal truths, it abolishes all religion, and all morality, instead of constituting them on a new basis; it therefore acts in contradiction to all past historical experience" (489), Felix states,

> But it would be fool's work to batter down a pump only because a better might be made, when you had no machinery ready for a new one: it be wicked work, if villages lost their crops by it. Now the only safe way...is not by any attempt to do away directly with the actually existing class distinctions and advantages, as if everybody could have the same sort of work, or lead the same sort of life (which none of my hearers are stupid enough to suppose), but by the turning of Class Interests into Class Functions or duties.[30]

Felix's attitude is what Marx and Engels would describe as Conservative or Bourgeois socialism:

> The Socialistic bourgeois want all the advantages of modern social conditions without the struggles and dangers necessarily resulting therefrom. They desire the existing state of society minus its revolutionary and disintegrating elements.... In requiring the proletariat to carry out such a system...it but requires in reality, that the proletariat should remain within the bounds of existing society, but should cast away all its hateful ideas concerning the bourgeoisie. (496)

For Felix, the need to cast away anger rests on the need to preserve "the common estate of society," what he calls "that treasure of knowledge, science, poetry.... This is something distinct from the indulgences of luxury and the pursuit of vain finery; and one of the hardships in the lot of working men is that they have been for the most part shut out from sharing in this treasure."[31] Such exclusion is the tragedy of Mr. Dagley's darkness—his exclusion, except for those few Biblical verses on Sunday, from participating in the give-and-take of culture and the construction of history.

But, Marx and Engels seem to respond: "That culture, the loss of which he laments, is, for the enormous majority, a mere training to act as a machine," an opportunity to "sell themselves piece-meal," to become "an appendage of the machine," "slaves of the bourgeois class" (478–79), and, finally, "The proletarians have nothing to lose but their chains. They have a world to win" (500). In contrast to this call for revolutionary action, Felix calls for reform born of social responsibility and education.

According to Haight, Eliot's "family would have been surprised to know how thoroughly conservative Marian had become. The revolutionary sentiments of those years in the Strand were gone forever."[32] Similarly, Bernard Semmel narrates Eliot's intellectual biography as though she embraced one belief system after another—first, Evangelical Calvinism, then freethinking followed by determinist phrenology, then Comtean positivism followed by Feuerbachian humanism, and finally, the traditional politics of inheritance of Burke and the conservatives.[33] Semmel evokes an either/or paradigm, but I am uncomfortable charting Eliot's intellectual development as a linear movement from radical to conservative. Rather than such fragmentation and linearity, a fluid both/and paradigm seems more appropriate, a recursive process of selecting and fusing from a variety of sources.

In her essay "Margaret Fuller and Mary Wollstonecraft" (1855), Eliot objected to an essentialist approach to women's nature, writing that "some of the best things she [Fuller] says are on the folly of absolute definitions of woman's nature and absolute demarcations of woman's mission. 'Nature,' she says, 'seems to delight in varying the arrangements, as if to show that she will be fettered by no rule; and we must admit the same varieties that she admits.'"[34] Eliot will be fettered by no labels. Rather than call her a Wordsworthian, a Comtean, or a Marxist, a more productive approach is to realize the significance of Eliot's innumerable scenes of reading. In her subsequent scenes of writing she transposed and orchestrated multiple and diverse ideologies into novelistic discourse where conflicting social and political voices speak and respond to one another. Subverting the very essence of labels like "conservative," "radical," "wife," "mother," and "writer," Eliot seemed to delight in varying the arrangements as she struggled to disrupt and expand the effects of discourse and broaden participation in creating culture and the possibilities of experience.

Reading Maggie Reading

> *To read George Eliot attentively is to become aware how little one knows about her. It is also to become aware of the credulity, not very creditable to one's insight, with which, half consciously and partly maliciously, one had accepted the late Victorian version of a deluded woman who held phantom sway over subjects even more deluded than herself.*
>
> Virginia Woolf
> "George Eliot"

In her book *George Eliot*, Kristin Brady shares Virginia Woolf's impression that we hardly know George Eliot. Brady recalls Charles Bray's phrenological conclusions that Eliot was "not fitted to stand alone" and in need of "some one to lean upon," and she quotes William Barry and Edmund Gosse who referred to Eliot as a "pythoness."[1] Brady demonstrates how Bray's pseudoscientific ideas were adopted by such prominent scholars as Gordon S. Haight, Sandra M. Gilbert and Susan Gubar. In Haight's narrative, rather than a strong and independent writer, Eliot became a woman writing by default because she was too ugly to find a husband to lean upon.[2] In Gilbert and Gubar's narrative, Eliot's schizophrenic sense of fragmentation resulted in a female power and creativity deformed by self-hatred.[3]

It comes as no surprise, then, that such critical approaches to Eliot's life inform discussions of her fiction as well. For example, Nina Auerbach, viewing witchcraft in the traditional terms of demonism and a smothering sexuality, claims that the demonism of Maggie Tulliver is planted in her very womanliness. Maggie's "primordially feminine hunger for love is at one with her instinct to kill and to die."[4] As Susan Fraiman notes, Auerbach's essay links Maggie to witches and other types of the monstrous female without examining their social meaning and operation, and "the result is almost to reify Maggie the witch as evil."[5] Whether focusing on Maggie's weakness or power to terrorize, there has been a tendency to pathologize both Maggie and her author.

Yet, as Brady argues, the primary texts surrounding Eliot's life and work invite different readings, and we find such readings beginning especially with the criticism of Margaret Homans, Mary Jacobus and Nancy K. Miller in 1981.[6] In the spirit of such difference, this chapter argues that in *The Mill on the Floss* Eliot tells us something about nineteenth-century female resistance and agency through the many scenes of reading that occur in the novel. Through the representation of Maggie Tulliver as an avid reader, Eliot evokes the agency of her own experiences with books which enabled her to perform a number of subversive repetitions in her life and writing.

All of Maggie's books come to her through men—her father, brother, Bob Jakin, and Philip Wakem—and can be grouped roughly into four categories: sacred texts of the Church, travel books, books comprising a classical education, and literature. In spite of the fact that these books construct the female in a negative and reductive manner, I argue that their great number and diversity allow Maggie to question authority, refuse conventional ways of being female, and make decisions different from those socially prescribed for women. In examining Maggie's relationship with books, I give special attention to Daniel Defoe's *The History of the Devil,* Thomas à Kempis's *The Imitation of Christ,* and Germaine de Staël's *Corinne or Italy.*

The second time we meet her, Maggie Tulliver sits "on a low stool close by the fire with a large book open on her lap."[7] The book is Defoe's *History of the Devil,* a satiric attack on women as devils, old hags and witches, and it was published in 1726, one year before the last official witch burning took place in Scotland.[8] Throughout *The Mill on the Floss* Maggie is repeatedly associated with witches in her early retreats to the worm-eaten floors and cobwebs of the attic, her fetish, her rebelliousness, her dark beauty, sensuality, wisdom and deviance, her social ostracism, and death by drowning. Early in the narrative she is described as "looking like a small Medusa with her snakes cropped," "a gypsy," and "whirling like a Pythoness."

However, between the time of Defoe's text and *The Mill on the Floss*, a new attitude toward witches emerged, and this new attitude is important in understanding the witch motif in *The Mill*. Whereas in the sixteenth and seventeenth centuries witches were persecuted and executed and in the eighteenth century rationalists denied that witchcraft ever existed, Romanticism in general and Walter Scott's *Letters on Demonology and Witchcraft* (1830) in particular believed that witches had been misunderstood and mistreated.[9] Scott ends his *Letters* by writing:

> There remains hope, however, that the grosser faults of our ancestors are now out of date; and that whatever follies the present race may be guilty of, the sense of humanity is too universally spread to permit them to think of tormenting wretches till they confess what is impossible, and then burning them for their pains.[10]

A passage from one of Eliot's essays "The Influence of Rationalism" suggests that she felt the same way. Eliot wrote of the "torturing, drowning, or burning the innocent":

> Mr Lecky shows clearly that dogmatic protestantism...would have felt it shame to be a whit behind Catholicism in severity against the devil's servants. Luther's sentiment was that he would not suffer a witch to live (he was not much more merciful to Jews); and, in spite of his fondness for children, believing a certain child to have been begotten by the devil, he recommended the parents to throw it into the river.... [T]he Scotch puritans...surpassed all Christians before them in the elaborate ingenuity of the tortures they applied for the discovery of witchcraft and sorcery, and did their utmost to prove that if Scotch Calvinism was the true religion, the chief "note" of the true religion was cruelty. It is hardly an endurable task to read the story of their doings; thoroughly to imagine them as a past reality is already a sort of torture.[11]

Eliot's inclusion in *The Mill on the Floss* of Defoe's text on devils and witches, the dialogue surrounding the picture of swimming a witch in the novel's first pages, Maggie's witchy ways, and the novel's closure all provide a framework which invites association with witches. The swimming test frame and running witch motif evoke this other historical narrative, lurking in the background, in the shadows, thinly veiled by the overlying structure of the novel. A brief overview of the persecution of women as witches will help in appreciating the encounter between Maggie and the story of the witch.

The major persecution of women as witches occurred in Europe between 1560 and 1760. Jeffrey B. Russell contends that this virulent outbreak of misogyny was fed by Western dualism, the Classical literary tradition, the Hebrew religion, and the misogynist tradition deeply inherent in Christianity.[12] Several Biblical passages demand the torture and murder of women as witches.[13] Anne Llewellyn Barstow estimates that about 200,000 were accused of witchcraft and 100,000 executed, and, on average, 80 percent of the accused and 85 percent of those executed were women. She writes that these statistics "document an intentional mass murder of women" and to ignore or put the statistics aside is to deny the "most persistent fact about the persecutions."[14] In reading the archival studies which emerged around 1965, Barstow notes three factors: the lack of gender analysis in previous scholarship, the high level of physical and gratuitous violence in the torture and executions, and the sexual nature of that violence.

Some of the women were, like Maggie Tulliver, wise women who were quarrelsome, independent-minded, passionate, and outspoken. As such, they represented a political, religious and sexual threat to the Protestant and Catholic churches as well as the state. Barbara Ehrenreich and Deirdre English note that "there is evidence that women accused of being witches did meet locally in small groups and that these groups came together in crowds of hundreds or thousands on festival days."[15] In contrast to the Church's anti-empiricist approach, witch-healers were active inquirers into material existence. For instance, they used ergot for labor·pain in opposition to the Church's claim that labor pain was God's punishment for Eve's original sin. In the roles of midwives, healers, and counselors, their work overlapped in dangerous and threatening ways with that of the priest and doctor. In addition, due to demographic changes in the sixteenth century, perhaps as many as 40 percent of women lived without the legal and social protection of husbands, and these independent women made easy targets.[16] At the end of *The Mill on the Floss*, Maggie, too, is without the protection of father, brother or husband and experiences some of the same kind of alienation.

Because witches were seen as having some control over sexual matters like potency, fertility, and abortion, the church determined to wrest this power to affect the birth rate from them."[17] For nearly three centuries *The Malleus Maleficarum*—commissioned by Pope

Innocent VIII, written by two Dominican priests, and published in 1486—was used as the how-to manual for the identification, torture, and punishment of women as witches.[18] Its misogyny may well be unparalleled. For example, the authors, Heinrich Kramer and James Sprenger, declare that "All wickedness is but little to the wickedness of a woman.... What else is woman but a foe to friendship, an inescapable punishment, a necessary evil," and "it should be noted that there was a defect in the formation of the first woman, since she was formed from a bent rib.... And all this is indicated by the etymology of the word; for *Femina* comes from *Fe* and *Minus*, since she is ever weaker to hold and preserve the faith."[19]

Immediately after its publication, a whole class of men appeared in Europe whose sole employment was to discover and burn witches, and because the "common prickers" received a fee for each witch discovered, persecution became lucrative. In "The Influence of Rationalism" Eliot writes that it was the "regular profession of men called 'prickers' to thrust long pins into the body of a suspected witch in order to detect the insensible spot which was the infallible sign of her guilt."[20] Since few if any bodies were without blemishes—moles, warts, birthmarks, pimples, pockmarks, cysts—the search for witch marks seldom failed.[21]

In sum, according to *The Malleus,* "woman" is defectively formed from a bent rib, feeble, intellectually like a child, consumed with an insatiable carnal lust, wicked and always deceptive, an "evil of nature painted with fair colors" with a slippery tongue. In terms of her gait, posture, and habit, woman is the "vanity of vanities." Referring to the *Malleus* as a "fantastic document," and to its impact as "immediate and frightful," Ilza Veith writes that "it soon became an international 'best-seller' throughout Europe"[22] Influential books like *The Malleus Maleficarum* and *The History of the Devil* conflated women with the devil and depravity, and Ehrenreich and English argue that the "witch-hunts left a lasting effect: An aspect of the female has ever since been associated with the witch, and an aura of contamination has remained...."[23] In *The Mill on the Floss* Eliot subversively repeats this sinister construction of the witch in order to transform it into a woman curious, strong, wise, sensual and beautiful. Using the symbolic power of the swimming test and weaving it throughout the narrative, Eliot repeats it with a difference. In her threatening defiance of the intimidated and submissive woman,

Maggie is like a witch, and she is constrained by the invisible but equally overpowering ropes of gender, family, and tradition.

Clearly, at the age of nine, Maggie is the most intelligent member of her family. Ironically, while she sits with the book open on her lap, her father and his friend Mr. Riley discuss her brother Tom who will receive the formal education Maggie is denied. Yet, as Maggie's father tells Mr. Riley, Tom is "slow with his tongue" and "reads but poorly, and can't abide the books, and spells all wrong" (18). In contrast, Maggie "can read almost as well as the parson" and "understands what one's talking about so as never was. And you should hear her read— straight off, as if she knowed it all beforehand. And allays at her book!" (12, 15). Maggie's mother fails to understand or acknowledge any value in her precocity; instead, she continually complains about Maggie's appearance and behavior, constructing her as "a wild thing," "half an idiot," and "a Bedlam creatur," whose "brown skin makes her look like a mulatter." Rather than giving her daughter confidence and self-validation, Mrs. Tulliver focuses on skin color, hair and clothes and scolds and seems to dislike Maggie.

While Mr. Riley and Maggie look at the picture of the swimming test together, Maggie explains, "It's a dreadful picture, isn't it? But I can't help looking at it. That old woman in the water's a witch— they've put her in to find out whether she's a witch or no, and if she swims she's a witch, and if she's drowned—and killed, you know— she's innocent, and not a witch, but only a poor silly old woman. But what good would it do her then, you know, when she was drowned?" (16). An active questioning reader, Maggie discerns the fatal double bind of the swimming test.[24]

Mr. Riley refers to *The History of the Devil* as not quite the right book for a little girl, wondering how it came into the house. Mr. Tulliver, who had been listening with "petrifying wonder," explains, "Why, it's one o' the books I bought at Partridge's sale. They was all bound alike—it's a good binding, you see—and I thought they'd be all good books" (16). Maggie has read *The History of the Devil* many times, but what does she learn from reading and rereading this text? How does Defoe's text work to construct Maggie as "female," and how does she resist this construction?

Throughout the first half of *The History of the Devil,* Defoe discusses his problems with Milton's epic saying, "Mr Milton was a good poet, but a bad historian" (92). One example concerns Satan's rebellion. The difficulty for anyone writing on the origins of evil is how "the devil came to fall.... How the spotless seraphic nature could receive infection?" (84). Defoe also points out problematic aspects of the Biblical story: how Satan could know of the creation of Adam and the place of his creation; and the "strange fate of sleeping in Paradise! that whereas we have notice but of two sleeps there, that in one a woman should go out of him, and in the other, the Devil should come into her" (120); why God accepted Abel's offering and not Cain's, Cain being the older son (128, 130); and how Noah left rules behind when there were no letters or writing (177). Defoe's disrespectful tone and questioning of authority serve as precedent and model for Maggie, a model she may even turn upon Defoe himself and other texts and experiences.

While this questioning of authority is important, in other ways Defoe's text is detrimental to Maggie as a woman reader. If Maggie identifies with the narrative voice, she must despise her own body. Defoe's selection and manner of discussing old testament female figures in the first half, and his frequent contemptuous discussion of witches and old hags in the second section of the book result—in spite of the "humor"—in a content and tone bitterly misogynist. At one point he states that an old woman is the devil's "favourite instrument" (245). "Modern naturalists," Defoe observes, "especially some who have not so large a charity for the fair sex, as I have, tells (*sic*) us, that as soon as ever Satan saw the woman...he saw evidently that she was the best formed creature to make a tool of, and the best to make a hypocrite of, that could be made" (70). Notwithstanding one or two brief references, the women in *The History of the Devil* are all bad women, from Eve to Lot's two daughters who "go and lie with their own father; the Devil telling them, doubtless, how to do it, by intoxicating his head with wine" (179), from Solomon's seraglio of whores, seven hundred of whom are princesses, to over twenty direct textual references to women as devils and witches; in a word, "the walking devils that we have generally among us, are of the female sex; whether it be that the Devil finds less difficulty to manage them, or that he lives quieter with them, or that they are fitter for his business than the men..." (337). In spite of claims for the cleverness of such satire or critical excuses that the book was written during Defoe's "crabbed old age," his treatment of women in general and old women in particular stands squarely in the tradition of *The Malleus Maleficarum*.

Nothing new, Defoe's misogynist discourse repeats in order to consolidate the old myth of feminine evil. Maggie has no mentor or feminist filter to guide her through Defoe's moral contradictions, no access to a library, to a critical heritage that would balance Defoe's misogyny with biographical and historical explanations or introduce her to his more progressive views toward women, marriage and independence. As mediators between consciousness and body, both Defoe and her family tell Maggie her body is bad, inferior, and out of control. A strong, intelligent mind in a female body—"a small mistake of nature" (12)—causes disease and divisiveness and poses a threat to the established order of power, wealth, and male identity. Nevertheless, Maggie learns from Defoe's frequent challenges to traditional authority—Defoe's challenge of Milton's authority to explain the source of evil, for example—and she increasingly appropriates this critical method of reading, applying it to Defoe himself, other texts, and her family and community.

Toward the close of Maggie's first scene of reading, Mr. Riley, in "an admonitory patronizing tone" with his "fat hands," "waxen eyelids and high-arched eyebrows," advises Maggie to put by *The History of the Devil* and read some prettier book:

> "Have you no prettier books?"
>
> "O yes...I've got 'Æsop's Fables,' and a book about Kangaroos and things and the 'Pilgrim's Progress.'"...
>
> "Ah, a beautiful book," said Mr Riley; "you can't read a better."
>
> "Well, but there's a great deal about the devil in that," said Maggie, triumphantly, "and I'll show you the picture of him in his true shape, as he fought with Christian."

Embarrassed, her father says "Go, Go!...It is as I thought—the child 'ull learn more mischief nor good wi' the books. Go, go and see after your mother" (17). Maggie's voice is stilled. Mrs. Tulliver enters the room and, hearing her ask a question, stifles her a second time: "Hush Maggie, for shame of you, asking questions and chattering" (21). But even in such an obtuse atmosphere, she cannot keep still. Her reading and intimacy with books, her inquiring mind and quick responses displace her from the positions of daughter and young lady. An unspoken fear underlies her father's embarrassment, Riley's patronizing disapproval, and her mother's dislike, a fear of what is strange and threatening—what is witchlike—in Maggie.

Besides Defoe's *The History of the Devil,* the Tulliver library includes *Æsop's Fables, Animated Nature, Pilgrim's Progress,* the Bible, *Holy Living and Dying, Pug's Tour Through Europe; or the Travell'd Monkey,* and a Catechism of Geography, and Maggie frequently initiates conversations about these books. When she visits the mill, "she conversed with the miller Luke, to whom she was very communicative, wishing him to think well of her understanding, as her father did" (260). She tries to interest Luke in her books, first with *Pug's Tour of Europe,* saying, "that would tell you all about the different sorts of people in the world"; then she tries *Animated Nature,* referring to elephants, kangaroos, the civet cat and sun-fish and a bird which sits upon its tail. She explains, "There are countries full of those creatures, instead of horses and cows, you know. Shouldn't you like to know about them, Luke?" But Luke seems to have no interest in the people and creatures outside the mill; in fact, he tells Maggie, "That's what brings folks to the gallows—knowin' everything but what they'n got to get their bread by. An' they're mostly lies, I think, what's printed i' the books..." (27).

When Maggie runs away to Dunlow Common, she tells the gypsies,

> I should have liked to bring my books with me, but I came away in a hurry, you know. But I can tell you almost everything there is in my books, I've read them so many times.... I can tell you something about Geography—that's about the world we live in—very useful and interesting. Did you ever hear about Columbus? (95)

The narrator ironically comments, "Maggie Tulliver, you perceive, was by no means that well-trained, well-informed young person that a small female of eight or nine necessarily is in these days: she had only been to school a year at St Ogg's, and had so few books that she sometimes read the dictionary" (98). Being the thorough reader that she is, however, Maggie makes the most of reading the dictionary, and the results are carefully noted later in the narrative.

In spite of their scarcity and quality and in spite of the absence of anyone with whom she can adequately discuss them, Maggie actively engages with her books: her psyche captures, mixes, and re-forms the events, ideas and characters in an ongoing and dynamic exchange. Over time, this discursive engagement increasingly positions her differently than other female characters like her mother, aunts, or cousin Lucy Deane. In this different space, Maggie confronts and analyzes multiple and diverse perspectives and acquires knowledge and uncommon desires. She wants to master books, to argue and speculate about great ideas, and to create narratives, but Tom says, "My sister Maggie is always wanting to tell me stories—but they're stupid things. Girls stories always are" (144). When Tom bemoans his lack of accounting knowledge, Maggie, referring to Walter Scott's *Guy Mannering,* answers, "O what a pity we haven't got Dominie Sampson.... If he had taught me book-keeping by double entry and after the Italian method, as he did Lucy Bertram, I could teach you" (204). But instead of impressing, the female intellect irritates those forced to confront it. Tom harshly responds, "*You* teach! Yes, I daresay. That's always the tone you take.... But it's always the same.... You're always setting yourself up above me and every one else, and I've wanted to tell you about it several times" (204). With Tom, like Mr. Riley, Luke and the Gypsies, Maggie fails to gain respect. Her sharp and witty mind does not harmonize with socially acceptable notions of femininity.

Visiting Tom at school at King's Lorton and upon entering the study, Maggie exclaims, "O, what books!... How I should like to have as many books as that" (128). When she offers to help Tom with Euclid, he says, "*You* help me, you silly little thing!... Girls never learn such things. They're too silly." She informs him there are Latin words in the dictionary—"bonus," a gift, for example. He says, "Now, you're just wrong there.... You think you're very wise! But 'bonus' means 'good'...." Maggie counters, "Well, that's no reason why it shouldn't mean 'gift'.... It may mean several things—almost every word does" [original emphasis] (127). That time spent with the dictionary provides Maggie with a sense of the play of language, its ambiguity and multiplicity. Tom, in contrast, accepts without question an absolute and transparent correspondence between word and reality. The narrator refers to Tom's "exceptional dulness," and "Mr. Stelling was convinced that a boy so stupid at signs and abstractions must be stupid at everything else" (148). Although Eliot has repeatedly made it clear that Maggie has the intellectual aptitude for Latin and geometry, Stelling—who knows Maggie as well as

Tom—responds to Tom's question, "Girls can't do Euclid: can they, sir?" by saying in Maggie's presence, "They can pick up a little of everything, I daresay.... They've a great deal of superficial cleverness, but they couldn't go far into anything. They're quick and shallow" (132).

Coming downstairs for the first time after her father's bankruptcy, Maggie's eyes go immediately "to the place where the bookcase had hung; there was nothing now but the oblong unfaded space on the wall, and below it the small table with the Bible and the few other books." She burst out, "Where are the books? I thought my uncle Glegg said he would buy them." Tom answers with "a sort of desperate indifference, 'Why should they buy many books when they bought so little furniture?'" (209). Considering the myopic nature of Maggie's books, and yet the despair she feels when they are gone, one can only speculate about what she might have been and done with a different set of books.[25]

In spite of the sale, books continue to come to Maggie in a variety of odd ways. She still has her small collection of schoolbooks, but "Télémaque was mere bran; so were the hard dry questions of Christian Doctrine: there was no flavour in them—no strength" (250). She remembers Tom's schoolbooks, and for a time she fills the vacant days with Latin, geometry and logic, "feeling a gleam of triumph now and then that her understanding was quite equal to these peculiarly masculine studies" (251). But these books fail to explain her situation, and she "rebelled against her lot" (251).

Then, Bob Jakin brings Maggie a new bundle of books which contains *Beauties of the Spectator, Rasselas, Economy of Human Life, Letters on the Evidences, Doctrines, and Duties of the Christian Religion*, and Thomas à Kempis's *The Imitation of Christ*.[26] Discarding the Virgil, Euclid and Aldrich—"the wrinkled fruit of the tree of knowledge"—abandoning the "vain ambition" that motivated her to study these cornerstones of "masculine wisdom," Maggie now reads "eagerly and constantly in her three books, the Bible, Thomas à Kempis, and the 'Christian Year'" (256). Reading *The Imitation of Christ* provides a temporary distraction, a new perspective on earthly experience which condemns the flesh, the senses and the intellect, embracing instead renunciation and self-abasement. Because she has already been deprived of pleasurable experiences—music, affection, companionship and her library—Maggie has little to renounce; she only needs the philosophical framework that will make the deprivation appealing, good and meaningful.

From a materialist point of view *The Imitation of Christ* strikes one as alienating, narrow and absolutist; from a psychoanalytic point of view it appears obsessive and masochistic; yet, in *The Mill on the Floss* the narrator is not overtly critical. Maggie is desperately lonely when Bob brings her this book, and it provides a spiritual philosophy.[27] One of the most well known examples of fifteenth-century devotional literature, *The Imitation of Christ* counsels pure contemplation and submission, behavior which wins societal approval for Maggie. Throughout Thomas à Kempis one finds a negative attitude toward intellectual investigation and discursive contacts, and the text's condemnation of reading, discussion, and intellectual investigation appears—somewhat like the miller Luke's—seamless. Thomas à Kempis writes: "Certainly at the day of doom it shall not be asked of us what we have read but what we have done" (6); and "Verily he is prudent that deemeth all earthly things as stinking dung so that he may win Christ" (8). The divine presence in the text says, "Son, let not the fair and the subtle sayings of men move thee for the realm of God is not in word but in virtue. Take heed to my words.... Read never anything for thee to seem better taught or wiser" (185), "for what are words but words? they flee through the air but they hurt not a stone" (191); and "Son beware that thou dispute not of high matters...for they be incomprehensible to man's understanding" (223). The narrator orders the male reader to repeat the prescribed behavior with no difference, to imitate the message contained in this one text. The continual command to avoid words inadvertently acknowledges the threat posed by intellectual investigation and discursive contacts.

Regarding social contact, the narrator of *The Imitation of Christ* states: "Be rarely among young people and strange folks.... Be not familiar to any woman but generally commend all good women to God" (14). Here the female is excluded both as reader and as social and intellectual contact. About self-torture, he advises, "Unless thou do force to thyself, thou shalt never overcome vice" (45); "So much thou shalt profit as thou doest violence to thyself" (58); and if God "give pains and beatings it ought to be taken gladly: for all is done for our help, whatever he suffereth to come to us" (84). The narrator refers to himself and man in general as an "abject worm," "contemptible," "wretched flesh," and "my great filthiness," and advises the reader to "show thee so subject and so little that all men may go over thee and tread upon thee as upon mire of the street" (125). Thinking of Maggie's dissatisfaction and rebelliousness as a child—dipping her hair in water immediately after her mother curls it, cutting her hair, shoving Lucy into the mud, running away—it is unlikely she could ever permanently become the meek and servile person Thomas à Kempis has in mind. Still, as a young woman in morose circumstances, she welcomes and lives this discourse of self-abasement for three years.

Turning her looking glass to the wall, Maggie redirects her energy into denial of the sensual world and her developing body. Yet, the text marks with care a transformation in her appearance, a change foreshadowed in the novel's first book.[28] Throughout the text Maggie's dark skin is noted no less than fifteen times. Early in the novel her Aunt Pullet says in a pitying tone, "it's very bad luck, sister, as the gell should be so brown" (59). But as Maggie develops, the brown skin becomes part of her overall beauty. After the auction even Mrs. Tulliver "was getting fond of her tall, brown girl...and Maggie, in spite of her own ascetic wish to have no personal adornment, was obliged to give way to her mother about her hair, and submit to have the abundant black locks plaited into a coronet on the summit of her head" (257). When Stephen Guest first sees Maggie, he "could not conceal his astonishment at the sight of this tall dark-eyed nymph with her jet-black coronet of hair" (330). In its nobility and beauty, Maggie's body signifies quite differently from the earlier images of a "wild thing," "spitfire," "Skye terrier," "Shetland pony," and "rough, dark, overgrown puppy."

During her three-year Thomas à Kempis retreat, Maggie does enjoy the pleasure of walking outdoors, and it is during one such walk that she again meets Philip Wakem who becomes her new source of books: "You may see her now...her tall figure and old lavender gown visible through an hereditary black silk shawl.... With her dark colouring and jet crown surmounting her tall figure, she seems to have a sort of kinship with the grand Scotch firs" (263). As they walk together, Philip asks, "Have you many books? You were so fond of them when you were a little girl." Maggie answers, "No, I have given up books, except a very, very few" (269). On another such walk, Philip tells Maggie, "you are shutting yourself up in a narrow self-delusive fanaticism, which is only a way of escaping pain by starving into dulness all the highest powers of your nature" (288). Philip wants to continue meeting, but to do so Maggie must abandon the philosophy of Thomas à Kempis and deceive her father and brother. Meeting Philip, however, means new discursive contacts: new books and an opportunity to exercise her wit and conversation about literature, art, and music. Later in the story, when Maggie tells Lucy about the secret meetings with Philip, Lucy responds: "Ah, now I see how it is you know Shakespeare and everything, and have learned so much since you left school; which always seemed to me witchcraft before—part of your general uncanniness" (340).

The next thing we hear Maggie saying to Philip is

Take back your *Corinne*.... You were right in telling me she would do me no good; but you were wrong in thinking I should wish to be like her.... I didn't finish the book.... As soon as I came to the blond-haired young lady reading in the park, I shut it up, and determined to read no further.... If you could give me some story, now, where the dark woman triumphs, it would restore the balance. I want to avenge Rebecca and Flora MacIvor, and Minna and all the rest of the dark unhappy ones. (291–92)

Although she doesn't finish, Maggie does read most of the book—a full three quarters—more than enough to evaluate Corinne's situation. But why wouldn't she like this book—so different from Defoe and Thomas à Kempis—a romance and travelogue of Italy set in 1798–1803 written about "the most celebrated woman in Italy"?[29]

When first introduced, Corinne, as poet, musician, painter and sculptor, is being crowned with laurel in Rome as Italy's most exalted artist. This crowning links Corinne and Maggie as it resonates back to Maggie's "abundant black locks plaited into a coronet on the summit of her head." Corinne has published books, acts the part of Juliet and sings comic opera in Gozzi's *Figlia dell' aria* in Venice; she is a spectacular woman who has everything—youth, beauty, independent wealth, genius, wit and good friends. Why wouldn't Maggie like a book that is so highly critical of that conservative British strain that would restrict women to the narrow confines of domesticity, the same cruel strain of intolerance and prejudice that infects her brother Tom?

Corinne escapes women's social oppression only to internalize extreme forms of emotional oppression by falling fatally in love with

Oswald Lord Nelvil, peer of Scotland. Oswald is a man who, as Deborah Heller notes, represents the very prejudices of British society that Corinne has fled, and he is clearly Corinne's inferior.[30] Madame de Staël constructs Italy as a place favorable to female development, but Corinne takes full advantage of this space only to abandon it for love. Her creativity requires independence of mind, but she becomes increasingly dependent on Oswald. From the age of fifteen to twenty-one, she had lived in England, and she describes the experience as the "parching breath of malicious mediocrity." A friend advises Oswald, "A woman like that is not made to live in Wales.... [A]s lovable as Corinne is, I think like Thomas Walpole: *what do you do with that at home?*" [original emphasis] (133). Although she finds the idea of marriage distasteful, Corinne comes to a point—and Maggie reads to this low point—where she says to Oswald, "Do as you will with me, chain me to your fate like a slave" (289). Count d'Erfeuil says to Oswald, "perhaps you will bring her far more grief than ever I would, but women love to suffer as long as it is very romantic: so you are just right for her" (41). In the end Corinne dies of a "broken heart," and rather than the constraints placed upon women in British society, it is Corinne's masochism in the midst of Staël's Italian utopia that is so disappointing.

Corinne or Italy is not about the conflict of a woman of genius with society, but about her destruction by the ideology of romantic love. When Oswald comes to Italy, Corinne "falls in love," a love that not only destroys her, but a love the text assumes its implied reader will comprehend and accept. Madelyn Gutwirth observes: "Like *La Nouvelle Héloïse,* and nearly all of the literature of love, *Corinne or Italy* reaffirms the absolute primacy of couplehood, even as it breaks out to assert the right to female singularity."[31] Repeating some aspects of Staël's plot while refusing and inverting others, in *The Mill on the Floss* Eliot subverts "the literature of love."

In *Corinne or Italy* the blond-haired lady marries Oswald in the end, and while anticipating this may well be part of the reason Maggie refuses to finish, it is possible to interpret her refusal in a broader context. Maggie tells Philip that she wants to avenge Rebecca, Flora MacIvor, and Minna and all the rest of the dark unhappy ones. Her wish that dark women like Flora MacIvor triumph implies that such triumph involves more than romantic love.

Like the spirited Flora MacIvor who rejects Edward Waverley, Maggie rejects Philip Wakem and Stephen Guest, and she refuses to leave St. Ogg's. Maggie's character is constructed not as a character who desires a man to whom she can devote her life, but as a character "thirsty for all knowledge" (205). On the level of plot, such an interpretation emerges in decisions Maggie makes later in her own story, especially her decisions not to marry, not to live with her Aunt Glegg or her mother, and not to leave St. Ogg's, but to live independently and find employment. Excepting her three-year Thomas à Kempis retreat, Maggie constantly acts, and her ability to act is not enabled by the other characters who surround her, not by her mother, Riley, Tom or Stelling, but through her reading. When Maggie refuses to marry Stephen, he says, "Good God, Maggie!... you rave. How can you go back without marrying me? You don't know what will be said, dearest. You see nothing as it really is" (420). Before Maggie returns from Mudport, Tom thinks, "Would the next news be that she was married—or what? Probably that she was not married: Tom's mind was set to the expectation of the worst that could happen—not death, but disgrace" (425).

Speaking for the world's wife which "at St Ogg's, as elsewhere, always knew what to think," the narrator comments with ironic anger:

> If Miss Tulliver, after a few months of well-chosen travel, had returned as Mrs Stephen Guest—with a post-marital *trousseau,* and all the advantages possessed even by the most unwelcome wife of an only son, public opinion, which at St Ogg's, as elsewhere, always knew what to think, would have judged in strict consistency with those results.... Mr Stephen Guest had certainly not behaved well; but then, young men were liable to those sudden infatuated attachments...and, they say, he positively worships her...and he ran away with her in the boat quite against her will—and what could she do? She couldn't come back then: no one would have spoken to her; and how very well that maize-coloured satinette becomes her complexion!
>
> But the results, we know, were not of a kind to warrant this extenuation of the past. Maggie had returned without a *trousseau,* without a husband—in that degraded and outcast condition.... Could anything be more detestable?... Why, her own brother had turned her from his door.... It was to be hoped that she would go out of the neighbourhood—to America, or

anywhere—so as to purify the air of St Ogg's from the taint of her presence, extremely dangerous to daughters there! (431–32)

This complex passage demonstrates the power of discourse to construct experience—Maggie's boat trip can become two distinct narratives depending on her willingness or unwillingness to conform to the marriage plot. Moreover, in this passage the narrator performs a triple speak: 1) mimicking the voice of the world's wife—"could anything be more detestable?" 2) satirizing the triviality, cruelty, and hypocrisy of Tom and the world's wife in their sexism and blind reverence for matrimony, and 3) sympathizing with Maggie in her confrontation with this institutionalized coercion and condemnation. Referring to the power of language over reality, the narrator comments: "Even on the supposition that required the utmost stretch of belief—namely, that none of the things said about Miss Tulliver were true—still, since they *had* been said about her, they had cast an odour round her which must cause her to be shrunk from by every woman who had to take care of her own reputation—and of Society" [original emphasis] (444). The need to send Maggie away to purify the air, the idea that she has an infectious odor about her and that, as Miss Kirke says, "her mind must be of a quality with which she, for her part, could not risk *any* contact," illustrates the threat posed by Maggie's difference [original emphasis] (445).

The passages surrounding Maggie's decision not to marry Stephen Guest are particularly rich in irony, satire, and social critique. When she returns to St. Ogg's alone, she is treated as a "friendly bar-maid," but she refuses to leave: "I will not go away because people say false things of me. They shall learn to retract them" (437). When the flood comes, she rows the boat toward the mill to save her mother and brother, and even Tom is struck by her bravery: "It was not till Tom had pushed off...that the full meaning of what had happened rushed upon his mind.... They sat mutely gazing at each other: Maggie with eyes of intense life looking out from a weary, beaten face—Tom pale with a certain awe and humiliation" (458). Maggie's strong and independent character emerges clearly in these last scenes as her bravery appears equal to Bob's and greater than Tom's. In fact, Maggie finds Tom enclosed within the house, shouting from the attic.

The Mill on the Floss is not driven by who gets Maggie as the prize nor does it culminate in marriage. Maggie says, "I begin to think there can never come much happiness to me from loving: I have always had so much pain mingled with it. I wish I could make myself a world outside it, as men do" (363). However, Philip and Stephen both want to marry her, and both are stuck in the confines of masculine rivalry. Stephen finds Maggie irresistible (319); Philip sees the possession of Maggie as compensation for his deformity. But she refuses to be the object of Stephen's choice or restitution for Philip. While Philip's father characterizes her as "dangerous and unmanageable, eh?" Philip responds, "She's very tender and affectionate; and so simple—without the airs and petty contrivances other women have" (376). The Miss Guests, Stephen's sisters and the "glass of fashion" in St. Ogg's, took "some exception to Maggie's manners. She had a way of not assenting at once to the observations current in good society, and of saying that she didn't know whether those observations were true or not, which gave her an air of *gaucherie,* and impeded the even flow of conversation" [original emphasis] (351). There was something rather bold in Maggie's direct gaze, and something undefinably coarse in the style of her beauty (378). Maggie's ability to interrupt an easy flow in conversation lies in her dislocated perspective and subsequent capacity to create discomfort, challenge assumptions, and disrupt the status quo.

Reading Maggie reading, we see her move through her father's haphazard library, the sacred books of the Church, her brother's classical schoolbooks, and the literature Philip provides. When we first meet her, Maggie has already spent a great deal of time with her books, and from the beginning, she is an active and questioning reader. Each of the texts discussed—*The History of the Devil, The Imitation of Christ* and *Corinne or Italy*—is imbued with the discourses of defiance, religious renunciation, and romantic love respectively, and, thus, each conveys a different world view. Defoe continually questions traditional figures of authority, and, likewise, Maggie challenges Mr. Riley's authority to tell her what books to read. As a young girl and a young woman, she refuses to comply with societal structures regarding appropriate feminine behavior. She meets Philip in the Red Deeps, she refuses to marry Philip or Stephen, and she refuses to go away. Her power as a reader reveals itself in her refusal to finish *Corinne or Italy,* an act symbolizing the possibility of refusing certain plots in order to imagine others. However, it is just at this point that Maggie's reading stops. While the books Maggie reads appear to become less and less inimical to women, paradoxically they become more pernicious as Defoe's explicit misogyny is replaced by Thomas à Kempis's persuasive rhetoric masking its underlying masochism, replaced, in turn, by Staël's Italian utopia obscuring Corinne's total entrapment by and sacrifice to the ideology of romantic love.

For many, *The Mill*'s ending does not signify any kind of success. Dr. Kenn has told Maggie she must leave St. Ogg's as "her stay was a source of discord between himself and his parishioners, that was likely to obstruct his usefulness as a clergyman" (451). She has Stephen's letter on the table and the words of Thomas à Kempis by memory, and she moves back and forth from one to the other. Doomed to endlessly repeat the cycle of confronting and refusing the discourses of renunciation and romance—"the old shadowy enemies that were for ever slain and rising again"—Maggie despairs (449).

In this setting, discursive agency cannot lead to a happy ending in any conventional sense; the various books Maggie reads will not provide a key to total release. However, the measure of her difference from the shallowness of her mother and aunts, Tom's androcentrism, Lucy's passivity, and the prejudice of Stephen's sisters is a measure of agency. While a limited kind of agency, Maggie's movement to the very margins and beyond of the St. Ogg's community marks a feminist struggle for a new center, a new space within which to create a world outside of subordination, renunciation, and the ideology of romantic love. Jacobus writes that Maggie is Eliot's text here, "a 'dead' language which thereby gives all the greater scope to authorial imaginings, making it possible for the writer to come into being."[32] After a spectacular rescue and reunion with Tom, Maggie drowns, then, proving her courage and innocence, concluding the witch framework initiated in the opening pages, and, as Jacobus argues, freeing her creator. Through the reading of numerous and conflicting texts, Maggie is able to dis-identify with the value system of her family and community, and in her intelligent, brave and witchy ways, she repeats to subvert traditional modes of femininity. In the end Maggie dies so that Eliot can continue to write, and in the void, in the empty space of her drowning, readers begin to imagine other possibilities.

Voice and Visibility in Charlotte Brontë

> *We do not hesitate to say that the tone of mind
> and thought which has overthrown authority
> and violated every code human and divine
> abroad, and fostered Chartism and rebellion
> at home, is the same which has also written
> Jane Eyre.*
>
> Elizabeth Rigby
> *Quarterly Review, 1848*

> *We would rather Winny would not read such
> excruciating novels as* Jane Eyre. *If you could
> get her Jane Austen's stories, or Miss Mulock's
> out of the library, we should be very glad. And
> for my own part, I wish she would read
> biography, history and poetry, rather than any
> sort of novels.*
>
> William Dean Howells
> *Selected Letters*

In the first half of the nineteenth century, women's socio-political
condition worsened in England. In order to clarify and codify cultural
expectations regarding women's bodies, the law against abortion was
passed in 1803, and the law denying women the right to vote was
passed in 1823. The great majority of women were the responsibility
of a nearest male relative—a father, uncle, brother, or husband—and
they remained in such positions of dependence throughout their lives.
Carole Pateman comments, "Women were deprived of an economic
basis for independence by the separation of the workplace from the
household.... The legal and civil standing of married women reached
its nadir in the mid-nineteenth century."[1]

This chapter examines three aspects of this bleak and oppressive period in women's history. First, it provides an overview of the laws regarding women, marriage, and property. Second, it examines early scenes of reading in Charlotte Brontë's life which allowed her to challenge much of the rhetoric maintaining women's subordinate status. Third, it examines the publication of *Jane Eyre* in 1847, not as the subjective act of a culturally isolated and intuitive genius, but as a thorough analysis and critique of male privilege and the patriarchal powers concealed in traditional romance. Rather than ahistorical and depoliticized texts, as Sally Shuttleworth argues, Brontë's fiction actively encodes the language, concerns and preoccupation of nineteenth-century social, psychological and economic thought, using individual characters to explore wider social issues and processes. In Brontë's characterization, contemporary political debates actively inform the individual psyche, and, far from revealing the inner secrets of essential selfhood, Brontë reveals how "selfhood" is only constructed in the experiences of social conflict.[2]

Critics such as Gayatri Spivak and Nancy Armstrong view *Jane Eyre* in the context of European imperial expansion and focus on the ways the text participates in and perpetuates hegemonic ideology.[3] This is important and illuminating work, but at the same time, this approach tends to dismiss *Jane Eyre*'s radical aspects. While Brontë did not have an enlightened consciousness regarding race, religion, or nation, she did realize the gross injustices of women's condition, especially those relating to physical appearance, education, and marriage. In spite of *Jane Eyre*'s inability to understand the imperialist project, the novel does understand and condemn the constraining effects of the early nineteenth-century colonization of the female body.

In the socio-political world surrounding *Jane Eyre* and without independent wealth, a woman's possibilities were limited to governess, needle woman, prostitute, author, or wife and mother. Most women received no formal education. The Return of Marriage Registers for 1851 shows that out of 154,000 women married, nearly 70,000 signed their names with marks.[4] No educational institutions existed for women until Queen's College was established in 1848 and Bedford College for Ladies in 1849, both founded to educate women as governesses. The constitution of Queen's College stipulated that it be administered entirely by men. Women were thought fit only for courtship, marriage and motherhood and were groomed accordingly, and the division of public and private space was strictly defined and enforced.

It was uncommon for women to attend public meetings, and it was unheard of for women to speak in public. When the American delegation arrived at the 1840 London Anti-Slavery Convention with women members, for example, it was seen as scandalous. For days the male participants debated the right of the American women to take part in the conference with clergymen contending that women's equality was against the will of God. Finally, the women were denied the right to speak, and Lucretia Coffin Mott and Elizabeth Cady Stanton, among others, were seated behind a curtained gallery.

An 1851 census revealed that "the number of females of marriageable age, in Great Britain, will always exceed the number of males of the same age to the extent of half a million."[5] Whether true or not, this statistic helped to make the marriage market highly competitive, and "young girls were trained for it like race horses."[6] In 1871 close to 90% of English women between forty-five and forty-nine were or had been married.[7] However, once married, the woman was the husband's property for life, a relationship referred to as "coverture." In his *Commentaries on the Laws of England*, the influential Sir William Blackstone described this relationship:

> By marriage, the husband and wife are one person in law: that is, the very being, or legal existence of the woman is suspended during the marriage, or at least is incorporated and consolidated into that of the husband; under whose wing, protection, and *cover*, she performs everything; and is therefore called...a *feme-covert*...her husband, [is called] her *baron*, or lord.[8]

These measures, Blackstone continued, protected women, "so great a favorite is the female sex of the law of England." Blackstone's rhetoric reveals how this inhibiting and restraining treatment of women was justified by calling it "protection."

The following quotation, taken from the *Reports of Cases Decided in the Court of Probate and in the Court for Divorce and Matrimonial Causes*, demonstrates how once instituted, such laws are maintained. In this particular case, Bostock v. Bostock, the wife, married in 1830, petitioned for dissolution of the marriage on the grounds of cruelty and abuse, but the judge dismissed the case saying:

The history of the married life of these parties is most melancholy; for thirty years they have been continually quarrelling; they have brought up a large family of children, upon whom the example of their parents cannot have failed to produce injurious effects; but I cannot, because they make each other unhappy, decree that they shall be separated. To use the language of Lord Stowell..., "Everybody must feel a wish to sever those...who cannot live together with any degree of harmony...but my situation does not allow me to indulge feelings, much less the first feelings, of an individual; the law has said that married persons shall not be legally separated upon the mere disinclination of one or both to cohabit together, the disinclination must be founded upon reasons which the law approves...."[9]

Repeating by reproducing the exact words of Lord Stowell—"married persons shall not be legally separated upon the mere disinclination of one or both to cohabit together"—the judge erases the woman's experience of thirty years of physical abuse. Through such repetitions and erasures, laws written, reviewed and retained by men can work to control and victimize women.

Caroline Sheridan Norton's story stands as the most notorious example of the ruinous effects of the laws concerning married women, and her story was retold in part by George Meredith in the novel *Diana of the Crossways* (1885). Known for her beauty, in 1827 at the age of nineteen Norton married George Norton, a Tory aristocrat and younger son. The couple barely knew each other, and from the beginning the marriage was a disaster. In 1835 while she was visiting a sister, her husband took their children from home, and during the following year brought an action of criminal conversation with his wife against Lord William Melbourne.[10] The case was dismissed, but the wife's reputation was permanently ruined; she could not see her children, and she was still tied to her husband by the unbreakable bond of marriage. She could not be represented by counsel at the trial. She could not sue. Her husband now claimed as his own all the earnings from her literary career.[11]

In 1855 Norton wrote *A Letter to the Queen on Lord Chancellor Cranworth's Marriage and Divorce Bill* accurately summarizing the legal condition of married women at the time. A married woman had no legal existence whether or not she was living with her husband. Her property was his property, and she could not keep her earnings. She could not make a will; she could not sign a lease or transact business, and she could not sue for libel. The husband could sue for restitution of conjugal rights and thus force her, as if a slave, to return to his home. She could not divorce him since the House of Lords in effect would not grant a divorce to her. She could not defend herself in a divorce proceeding, and she could not bind her husband to any agreement.[12]

The husband had the sole right to decide the family residence and where and how the children would be raised, including their religion. He had the right to physically abuse his wife in order to correct her. In Britain a wife could be jailed for refusing conjugal rights until 1884; husbands were allowed forcibly to imprison their wives in the home to obtain their rights until 1891. Once married, the woman was the husband's property for life. This condition of coverture was a condition often compared to that of slavery, and, according to Pateman, "perhaps the most graphic illustration of the continuity between slavery and marriage was that in England...wives could be sold at public auctions."[13] The perception of women informing this common law doctrine of coverture is, obviously, degrading, constructing living subjects as children and sexual objects if they obey the law and whores and criminals if they do not.

In 1849 about the condition of married women, the feminist activist Barbara Leigh Smith Bodichon commented that "there never was a tyranny so deeply felt yet borne so silently."[14] Bodichon's reflections on marriage predate those of John Stuart Mill, and she criticized Mill's *Principles of Political Economy* for overlooking important issues like the marriage contract and the laws concerning women. In 1854, as a corrective to Mill and predating his *The Subjection of Women* by fifteen years, Bodichon published the first edition of "A Brief Summary, in Plain Language, of the Most Important Laws Concerning Women: Together with a Few Observations Thereon." In 1855 she organized a small group of women to compose and circulate a petition in support of reform of women's property laws. This committee was the first organized feminist group in England and composed the core of what would become the Langham Place Circle.[15]

Bodichon's illegitimacy, her radical ideas, her friendship with the scandalous George Eliot, and her general style of living made her moral character highly questionable, and her "participation was often hidden by her coworkers to protect the reputation of various feminist undertakings."[16] Near the end of the century Bessie Parkes wrote that Smith's pamphlet, "A Brief Summary, in Plain Language," had been "the small end of the wedge which was to change the whole fabric of the law."[17] In this pamphlet Bodichon stated:

> A man and wife are one person in law; the wife loses all her rights as a single woman.... A woman's body belongs to her husband; she is in his custody, and he can enforce his right by a writ of *habeas corpus*.... She cannot be found guilty of stealing from her husband or of setting his house on fire, as they are one person in law. A husband and wife cannot be found guilty of conspiracy, as that offence cannot be committed unless there are two persons.[18]

Once engaged to be married, a woman had no legal right to her property, even her personal belongings. According to Bodichon: "not even her clothes, books, and household goods are her own, and any money which she earns can be robbed from her legally by her husband."[19] Comprehension of the degree and implications of this idea of "one person" is, perhaps, impossible from a late twentieth-century perspective. Nevertheless, the majority of women were forced to participate in the double bind of marriage as economic necessity and marriage as civil and economic death.

Charlotte Brontë was born in 1816, and the Brontë children were remarkably well informed in areas of current affairs. Certainly, Brontë knew of the legal and economic status of married women, and quotes from her letters reveal her disparaging attitude toward courtship and romance.

In 1839 she refused the second of four marriage proposals, writing, "I am certainly doomed to be an old maid. Never mind. I made up my mind to that fate ever since I was twelve years old."[20] In 1840 she wrote:

> Do not be over-persuaded to marry a man you can never respect—I do not say *love*; because, I think, if you can respect a person before marriage, moderate love at least will come after; and as to intense *passion,* I am convinced that is no desirable feeling. In the first place, it seldom or never meets with a requital; and, in the second place, if it did, the feeling would be only temporary: it would last the honeymoon, and then, perhaps, give place to disgust, or indifference worse, perhaps, than disgust. Certainly, this would be the case on the man's part.... I am tolerably well convinced that I shall never marry at all.

In 1845 she wrote:

> I know that if women wish to escape the stigma of husband-seeking, they must act and look like marble or clay—cold, expressionless, bloodless; for every appearance of feeling, of joy, sorrow, friendliness, antipathy, admiration, disgust, are alike construed by the world into the attempt to hook a husband. Never mind!... [D]o not too harshly repress sentiments and feelings excellent in themselves, because you fear that some puppy may fancy that you are letting them come out to fascinate him; do not condemn yourself to live only by halves, because if you showed too much animation some pragmatical thing in breeches might take it into his pate to imagine that you designed to dedicate your life to his inanity.

And, a year later she wrote:

> I speculate much on the existence of unmarried and never-to-be married women now-a-days; and I have already got to the point of considering that there is no more respectable character on this earth than an unmarried woman, who makes her own way through life quietly, perseveringly, without support of husband or brother....[21]

Displaying few if any illusions regarding courtship and marriage, Brontë identified issues and problems in her letter writing that would become the explicit and central concerns of her novels. Such issues include male attitudes toward women, the duration of sexual passion, and the value of women and work.

Without social status, wealth, or beauty and physically isolated at Haworth in northern England, Brontë was marginalized as a child and as a woman. In terms of her physical appearance, she was very small and said to be awkward. She was so near-sighted, she could not participate in games at school, and one friend wrote: "she always showed physical feebleness in every thing. She ate no animal food at school. It was about this time I told her she was very ugly"[22] However, in contrast to Brontë's awkward and weak physical body, Carol Bock identifies another Brontë as the young author, writing, printing, and binding books.

In order to preserve her writing, Brontë carefully sewed her manuscripts together into tiny bound volumes. Rather than a game of make-believe or a way to evade reality, the "attempt to imitate print through minuscule handwriting, the remarkable detail with which her title pages mock their real-life counterparts, the advertisements and reviews that simulate a literary climate in which the stories were supposedly received" demonstrate a deliberate attempt to recreate the powerful reality found through the experience of reading.[23] Irene Tayler begins her study of Charlotte and Emily Brontë with a corrective: "Charlotte and Emily Brontë are sometimes thought of as naifs or primitives, unschooled artists driven by native talent and emotional need, but largely innocent of the complex cultural and aesthetic movements of their time. Nothing could be less true."[24] The six Brontë children, according to Elizabeth Gaskell, took a "vivid interest" in local and foreign politics. They were not only voracious readers but would argue and discuss literary and political issues and incorporate contemporary characters and events into their own publications, repeating in their writing a number of conflicting ideologies.

Their father Patrick Brontë had attended Cambridge and considered the purchase of books a luxurious necessity. He kept a fair number in his library, including Homer and Virgil, Milton's works, Johnson's *Lives of the Poets,* Goldsmith's *History of Rome,* Hume's *History of England,* and Scott's *Life of Napoleon Bonaparte.* Thomas Bewick's *History of British Birds*, a book Jane Eyre reads, was a much-read book at the Haworth Parsonage.[25] Shuttleworth discusses Patrick Brontë's fascination with medical science and his collection of domestic medical texts, including William Buchan's *Domestic Medicine* and the secular Bible of the Brontë household, Thomas John Graham's *Modern Domestic Medicine.*[26] The children could also read their Aunt Branwell's subscription to *Fraser's Magazine.*

At thirteen Charlotte wrote in "The History of the Year 1829" that the family took two newspapers, the Tory *Leeds Intelligencer* and the Whig *Leeds Mercury*, and that a Mr. Driver lent them *Blackwood's Magazine* and the *John Bull*, "high Tory, very violent."[27] Brontë avidly read the *Leeds Intelligencer* and the *Leeds Mercury* from early childhood, and she "responded ardently to the political issues of the day." She followed the debates on Catholic emancipation and the Reform Bill in her early years, and the progress of the Chartists and the 1848 Revolution in France in her later years.[28] The "History" also includes a list of several plays the children wrote, and they brought out a magazine each month. In 1826 Patrick

Brontë gave Charlotte her mother's copy of Thomas à Kempis's *The Imitation of Christ*, the same book Maggie Tulliver embraces in *The Mill on the Floss*.

Lyndall Gordon notes Charlotte's reading widely in Virgil, Ovid, Scott, Byron, Edward Young, Cowper, and Ann Radcliffe along with habitual reading in the Bible. Still, her father's library contained no Fanny Burney, Mary Wollstonecraft, Mary Shelley or Jane Austen. Nor did Brontë borrow them from the Keighley Mechanics Institute, the public library four miles away.[29] The Mechanics Institute Library, a major source of books for the Brontë family, was primarily devoted to the natural sciences and philosophy, and there were lectures at the Institute on self development, practical topics like magnetism and geology, and historical topics like Napoleon. Attending such lectures may have formed part of Charlotte Brontë's education and social life.[30] The Brontë children may have also used the extensive library at Ponden House, the home of the Heatons who lived across the moor.

When Brontë arrived at Roe Head School in January 1832, she was well read, but behind in subjects like grammar and geography. When she left in June 1832, she was the school's top pupil. About these school days, Gaskell writes:

> She was an indefatigable student: constantly reading and learning; with a strong conviction of the necessity and value of education, very unusual in a girl of fifteen. She never lost a moment of time.... Then, at night, she was an invaluable story-teller, frightening [her friends] almost out of their wits as they lay in bed.[31]

The intellectual climate and countless literary activities of the Brontë household and her school performance attest to Charlotte's awareness of the importance of reading widely in various disciplines.

Brontë read in the classics, literature, science, biography, history, art, and current affairs, and her agency results from this contact with different points of view in one discipline and among disciplines. Seeing one discourse through the eyes of another, unresolvable contradictions emerge, and knowledge becomes an activity and often a struggle over interpretation and representation. According to Marcelle Thiébaux—and this is a decisive point—Brontë did not assimilate her sources tamely, but tended to improve them: "Unable to accept Milton's Eve, for example, as a charming inferior whipping up dulcet creams in Eden, Brontë revised her upward as a Titan, large and strong as the hills, one from whose body Titans would spring."[32] Refusing the legacy of female inferiority sustained in Milton's text, Brontë deliberately selected and recombined aspects of character and plot to fashion a distinct system of ideas and beliefs.

In 1842 at the age of twenty-six Charlotte left for Brussels to be introduced to an entirely new set of books in French and German. One particular incident helps to explain how she came to write her narratives with such energy, wit, and satire and with such a broad range of socio-ideological perspectives. In Brussels, her professor M. Heger employed a method of synthetic teaching:

> He would read to them various accounts of the same person or event, and make them notice the points of agreement and disagreement. Where they were different, he would make them seek the origin of that difference by causing them to examine well into the character and position of each separate writer, and how they would be likely to affect his concept of truth. For instance, take Cromwell. He would read Bossuet's description of him in the "Oraison Funèbre de la Reine d'Angleterre," and show how in this he was considered entirely from the religious point of view, as an instrument in the hands of God, pre-ordained to His work. Then he would make them read Guizot, and see how, in his view, Cromwell was endowed with the utmost power of free will, but governed by no higher motive than that of expediency; while Carlyle regarded him as a character regulated by a strong and conscientious desire to do the will of the Lord. Then he would desire them to remember that the Royalist and Commonwealth man had each their different opinions of the great Protector. And from these conflicting characters he would require them to sift and collect the elements of truth, and try to unite them into a perfect whole.
>
> This kind of exercise delighted Charlotte. It called into play her powers of analysis, which were extraordinary, and she very soon excelled in it.[33]

Heger's method reveals the varied religious, pragmatic, and political views of "Cromwell," uncovering the social languages present within one national language and between national languages such as English and French.

With her extraordinary powers of analysis, Brontë transposed a number of social languages into novelistic discourse. The logic of each social language embodied in the main characters in *Jane Eyre*—in Jane, John Reed, Brocklehurst, Helen Burns, Maria Temple, Blanche

Ingram, Rochester, and St. John Rivers—enacts a struggle with the others to control interpretation and meaning. Deliberately and repeatedly, the novel breaks with the conventions of romance and feminine performance, and the break was so radical for its time that some readers complained bitterly. In her 1848 review, Elizabeth Rigby wrote that Charlotte Brontë committed the "highest moral offence a novel writer can commit, that of making an unworthy character interesting in the eyes of the reader."[34] What Rigby judged as unworthy is Jane's powerful little body, possessing the energy and conviction to refuse degrading interpretations and travel to other places. Jane can move, change, and experiment with various roles and relationships, enacting a profound intervention in the nineteenth-century discourses which both represented and constituted female subjectivity.

Brontë's new aesthetic focusing on Jane's unattractive body and shrewd and discerning mind marked a radical departure from the beauties of conventional romance. In contrast to the bodies of Blanche Ingram and Rosamond Oliver, bodies created in the masculine fancy of traditional romance, Jane's body is small and plain, covered in sober colors with minimal ornamentation. In the end Jane's body all but disappears in the isolation of Ferndean and Rochester's blindness to be reconstituted through Jane's direction and interpretation. Unlearning a female legacy of abuse, subordination, and repressed desire, escaping the constraints of Victorian dress and the law, Jane's ability to analyze a situation and depart allows her to escape four increasingly subtle heterosexist situations. In these four situations the narrative shifts and dilates to critically display the classic patriarchy embodied in John Reed, Rev. Brocklehurst, Edward Rochester, and St. John Rivers.[35]

In the novel's first chapters, Jane reads Goldsmith's *History of Rome,* Bewick's *History of British Birds,* and Swift's *Gulliver's Travels.* Here is a rich scene of reading that surrounds and directs Jane's point of view. While her cousin John only throws books, Jane seizes the opportunity to borrow books from the Reed library, draw parallels, and refuse John's rule over her as wealthy cousin and male heir.

The first pages of *Jane Eyre* both present the relation between John and Jane and function as a form of closure on this kind of masochistic behavior. Brontë carefully notes that Jane had been "habitually obedient" to John Reed and also continually abused by him. The imperious young master demands of her body the posture and attitude of a slave. Telling the reader that she was "accustomed to John Reed's abuse," and "never had an idea of replying to it," Jane describes her body's usual response: "every nerve I had feared him, and every morsel of flesh on my bones shrank when he came near."

Jane has been reading behind the curtains when John strikes her "suddenly and strongly" and then throws her book, saying, "You have no business to take our books.... Now, I'll teach you to rummage my book-shelves: for they *are* mine" [original emphasis].[36] In the midst of this verbal and physical abuse, Jane clearly identifies the causal connection between her reading and her decision to rebel, saying to John, "Wicked and cruel boy!... You are like a murderer—you are like a slave-driver—you are like the Roman emperors!" To the reader she says, "I had read Goldsmith's *History of Rome,* and had formed my opinion of Nero, Caligula, &c. Also I had drawn parallels in silence, which I never thought thus to have declared aloud" (8).

The servants advise Jane to be humble, pleasant, and repentant so she might always have a home with the Reeds. If she is "passionate and rude," she will be sent away. Rejecting this "home," Jane becomes passionate and rude. She physically attacks John Reed. She has a fit. She speaks candidly to the doctor. After the red-room incident, she again hits John, this time in the nose with "as hard a blow as my knuckles could inflict" (27). She talks back. She tells her aunt Mrs. Reed that she is the bad one, hard-hearted and deceitful. Referred to as "bad animal," "rat," "mad cat," and "toad," hit upon repeatedly by John and Mrs. Reed, and mentally abused by the others, Jane has the good fortune of being pushed to extremes and retaliates with violent words and acts saying, "I was...winner of the field. It was the hardest battle I had fought, and the first victory I had gained" (40).

Jane arrives at this warrior-like stance through a physically inferior body without mother or father, a marginal class and gender status, and a subsequent contemptuous and indignant disposition. Her bird-like body, her identification with the cold and solitary freedom of birds, and her belief that *Gulliver's Travels* is a "narrative of facts" instill in Jane a desire to move and travel.

Using the rhetoric of Calvinistic hell-fire and damnation instead of physical abuse, the asylum director, Rev. Brocklehurst, replaces John Reed as the dominant sadistic male subject. Referring to Jane as a "castaway," "an interloper," and "an alien," he tells the other girls to "avoid her company, exclude her from your sports, and shut her out from your converse.... Teachers...punish her body to save her soul; if, indeed, salvation is possible" (76). While he lectures the Lowood orphans, his wife and daughters stand behind him. Jane comments: "They ought to have come a little sooner to have heard his lecture on dress, for they were splendidly attired in velvet, silk, and furs" (74). Through their clothing, wife and daughters signify prosperity, and they stand close by to mark Brocklehurst as successful and powerful.

Several female characters in *Jane Eyre* dress like the Brocklehurst women—Mrs. Reed and her daughter Georgiana, Lady Ingram and her daughter Blanche, and Rosamond Oliver. While the laws regarding the right to vote, to abortion, and to property in conjunction with the legal status of married women oppressed women in obvious ways, the fashionable clothing of the period oppressed women in more subtle and intimate ways. Moreover, while the laws applied to all women, such fashionable dress was only available to middle and upper class women, and this exclusivity had the effect of making Victorian dress a privilege and a sign of wealth and status, obscuring the negative consequences of wearing such costumes.

Structural underwear—corsets, petticoats and crinolines—altered the physical body by reducing or extending its natural shape. During the 1840s a stiffened petticoat of horsehair was worn to support wider skirts. In the 1850s hoops of whale bone were inserted into the petticoat. From this structure evolved first the whalebone and then the flexible-steel framework known as the crinoline, frequently called cages, a framework necessary to support the twenty yards of material often used in making a silk dress. One dress might easily weigh fifteen pounds.[37]

Duncan Crow writes that such fashion reflected the rejection of all forms of work by "ladies." The sleeve openings grew larger and larger, making the hand appear smaller, "a symbol of the helplessness and gentility of its owner." Skirts continued to expand until they became huge heavy domes, and walking "became like a perpetual struggle through shallow water." Tight lacing became fashionable, and to be able to manipulate the immense shawls correctly was the sure sign of a lady.[38] Helene Roberts writes that the crinoline with a circumference sometimes exceeding five yards literally transformed women into caged birds, and its light material posed the very real danger of inflammability.[39]

Deformed by corset and crinoline, the Victorian female body—heavy, expensive, immobilizing and potentially debilitating—functioned as secondary support and display for drapery. Like the bodies of Brocklehurst's women, it appeared heavy and static, a body without energy, with no visible legs or feet—a body incapable of quick movement. This object-body existed as a means to an aesthetic end, and any desire for power, influence, and agency was frustrated by the final effect. As Judith Butler explains, it is not enough to inquire into how women can be more fully represented in language and politics, but of how they are being produced and restrained by the very structures through which emancipation is sought, and then the process of production concealed and naturalized.[40] The complex Victorian system of body covering for women—from headgear, handbag, muff, shawl and gloves down through layers of silk and brocade, through whalebone or flexible steel petticoats to the chemises, pantelettes and, finally, corsets reinforced with wood or whalebone—was desired by the majority of women along with its real threat of bodily harm, bad health, and lack of mobility. As such, it represents a particularly poignant example of how female bodies were produced and quite literally restrained by structures through which emancipation was sought.[41]

While his family stands behind him properly encased in velvet, silk and furs, Brocklehurst works to enforce a strict uniformity in dress among the orphans. Because of their difference from his wife and daughters, the orphans necessitate a different kind of containment. Also, they serve as a threatening reminder to the Brocklehurst women of what could happen without patriarchal protection. Brocklehurst demands that Julia's naturally curly red hair be "cut off entirely," and after inspecting the others, he demands that all top-knots be cut. The many containment images operating in this section of *Jane Eyre* reveal the degree of the danger posed by female orphans, unacceptable women because they develop without the restraining influence of one or both parents. Brocklehurst provides the "proper" upbringing for these threatening women by providing a triple framework of confinement to control the space *around, on,* and *in* the female body: *around* with the high garden walls of Lowood Institution, "so high as to exclude every glimpse of prospect" (54); *on* with a homogenized dress code covering the bodies with coarse material, wool stockings, and plain close hair; and *in* with the ideology of Calvinism.

At Lowood the eighty bodies live communally: sometimes in twos in bed, sometimes in groups of four or in two rows down the sides of the school-room, six girls sharing one wash basin, all dressed the same, from nine to twenty years old. We lose sight of the toad-bird-rat-like Gateshead creature as Jane's body becomes part of this triply-confined collective body. Jane often uses the first person plural in describing her first months at Lowood, and this sense of a collective body marks the first of several major transformations Jane's body will undergo.

Along with the bodily changes, Jane's manner of interacting with others also changes. Rather than the physical abuse of the Reed family, Jane experiences the pleasure of physical affection, of hugs, kisses and the holding of hands, with both Helen Burns and Maria Temple. Jane also finds intellectual stimulation through these women who discuss history, science, French authors, and read Virgil in Latin. Enclosed within the safe space of Maria Temple's room, Helen's "soul sat on her lips, and language flowed" in "pure, full, fervid eloquence" (85). As well as being a means to personal agency, reading in this novel also brings women together collectively in relations of entrustment. Jane comes to love Maria Temple, and it is Temple—Jane's "mother, governess, and latterly, companion"—who Jane desires to please. She discovers a comfort and intellectual stimulation in these relationships, suggesting a type of female bonding apart from the conventional competition, conceit and jealousy conducive to heterosexism.

Because Maria Temple leaves, Jane also prepares to leave Lowood. Having learned the importance of external control, she actively takes steps to acquire another position. Before she leaves, Bessie visits, and through Bessie's comments Brontë explicitly marks another transformation in Jane's body: she has become "genteel enough" and looks like a "lady" in her black stuff dress (109). No longer a toad or one of Brocklehurst's orphans, Jane, having learned music, French, and art, has evolved into a school-mistress and governess.

In place of John Reed's physical violence or Brocklehurst's religious violence, Rochester actuates his control through virility and wealth. However, when he first appears on a "tall steed" with a "great dog" at his side, Rochester falls off the horse and is in need of Jane's assistance, immediately setting up the relation of dependence with which the novel ends. While Jane continues to sustain her cool intellectual distance, she is at the same time physically attracted to this man, excited by his conversation, and flattered by his attention. The attraction, however, is undercut by the text's persistent hesitation and ambivalence. As Adrienne Rich argues, their relationship will repeat the pattern of traditional romance with significant differences.[42]

One sign of Jane's attraction to Rochester is the change she perceives in her appearance the morning after his proposal. Looking at her face in the mirror, Jane "felt it was no longer plain: there was hope in its aspect, and life in its colour" (324). Rochester too perceives the change saying,

> "Jane, you look blooming, and smiling, and pretty...truly pretty this morning. Is this my pale, little elf? Is this my Mustard-Seed? This little sunny-faced girl with the dimpled cheek and rosy lips; the satin-smooth hazel hair, and the radiant hazel eyes?" (I had green eyes, reader; but you must excuse the mistake: for him they were new-dyed, I suppose). (325)

This is one of two times the novel marks Jane as pretty, but the parenthetical remark negates the effect, spotlighting both the fanciful nature of love's vision and the narrator's cold perspective. Moreover, the dimpled cheek, rosy lips and "hazel" eyes fail to satisfy Rochester: he promptly begins a complicated and expensive attempt to redo Jane's body into something more like the body of Blanche Ingram. He sends for the family jewels and says, "I will make the world acknowledge you a beauty, too." Jane becomes uneasy feeling that "he was either deluding himself, or trying to delude me" (326). About his passion she comments, "For a little while you will perhaps be as you are now,—a very little while; and then you will turn cool.... I suppose your love will effervesce in six months, or less. I have observed in books written by men, that period assigned as the farthest to which a husband's ardour extends" (327). Resisting Rochester's attempts at alteration, Jane recognizes the misapprehension of his warmth and whim.

But, deaf to her verbal responses, Rochester insists on taking Jane to the silk warehouse where he orders her to select half a dozen dresses. She responds,

I hated the business, I begged leave to defer it.... Glad was I to get him out of the silk warehouse, and then out of a jeweller's shop: the more he bought me, the more my cheek burned with a sense of annoyance and degradation. As we re-entered the carriage...I sat back feverish and fagged. (338)

Oblivious to her discomfort, Rochester patronizingly says, "it is your time now, little tyrant, but it will be mine presently; and when once I have fairly seized you...I'll just, figuratively speaking—attach you to a chain like this (touching his watch-guard)" (341). She refuses to kiss him after he sings to her, and he says "any other woman would have been melted to marrow at hearing such stanzas crooned in her praise" (344). Jane is careful not to melt. She persuades him to put off sending for the family jewels, and rather than six, she buys material for two dresses.

Even though Rochester tells Jane that hiring a mistress is the next worst thing to buying a slave—"both are often by nature, and always by position, inferior," after the failed marriage he offers Jane this "degrading" relationship (398). He argues, "you have neither relatives nor acquaintances whom you need fear to offend by living with me" (404). Knowing that she would become the successor to his French, Italian and German mistresses, knowing that the arrangement would lead to inequality and other kinds of abuse, Jane refuses his offer of a villa in France, escaping yet another exploitive situation.

After Jane's escape from Thornfield, Brontë's painstaking analysis of romantic love and its complicity with classic patriarchy continues and intensifies in Jane's relationship with St. John Rivers. Like Brocklehurst, St. John is a Calvinist, preaching the doctrines of election, predestination, and reprobation in his sermons. Jane describes him as a profound scholar and an extremely good looking man who dresses well with polished and gentleman-like manners. His face is like a Greek face, pure in outline with a classic nose, Athenian mouth and chin, large blue eyes, and a forehead, colorless as ivory, streaked by careless locks of fair hair (440).

Their relationship becomes increasingly tense and distrustful as St. John gradually gains a power over her: "When he said 'go,' I went; 'come,' I came; 'do this,' I did it. But I did not love my servitude" (508). He proposes marriage, and from his point of view this offer constitutes Jane's chance to become one of God's chosen few. He tells her: "God and nature intended you for a missionary's wife.... [Y]ou are formed for labour, not for love.... You shall be mine: I claim you—not for my pleasure, but for my Sovereign's service" (514). Although he claims her for service not pleasure, Jane feels certain that he would "scrupulously observe" all the forms of love (517), and she well understands the consequences: "If I join St. John, I abandon half myself: if I go to India, I go to premature death" (516).

Jane does agree to accompany him to India, but as a fellow missionary instead of his wife, but he does not "want a sister: a sister might any day be taken from me. I want a wife: the sole helpmeet I can influence efficiently in life, and retain absolutely till death" (518). However dramatic these last words appear, they accurately reflect the legal status of married women at the time. In a marriage contract with St. John, Jane would become subordinate in all matters and exchange her sexual and domestic service for his "protection."

Shocked by her refusal, St. John becomes sullen and outwardly cruel, telling her, "if you reject it, it is not me you deny, but God. Through my means, He opens to you a noble career: as my wife only can you enter upon it" (522). She says to Diana, "Would it not be strange, Die, to be chained for life to a man who regarded one but as a useful tool?... [Y]et, if forced to be his wife, I can imagine the possibility of conceiving an inevitable, strange, torturing kind of love for him.... In that case, my lot would become unspeakably wretched" (531). Through dialogue and commentary, the text dissects St. John's perspective and a number of female responses.

In contrast to Jane's relationship with St. John, her previous supportive, intellectual, and affectionate relation with Helen Burns and Maria Temple repeats itself with Diana and Mary Rivers, women Adrienne Rich calls "unmarried bluestockings" who delight in learning.[43] Together the three women read poetry, study German, and draw. The word "eloquent," used earlier to describe Helen Burns, appears again, and their discourse is described as being "witty," "pithy," and "original." Diana holds Jane's hand, puts her own hand on Jane's head, and they kiss. Jane is particularly attracted to Diana: "She possessed eyes whose gaze I delighted to encounter.... It was my nature to feel pleasure in yielding to an authority supported like hers..." (439). Other than Rochester, Diana is the only character to call Jane "pretty" saying, "Plain! You? Not at all. You are much too pretty, as well as too good, to be grilled alive in Calcutta" (530). Jane says,

If in our trio there was a superior and a leader, it was Diana. Physically, she far excelled me: she was handsome; she was vigorous. In her animal spirits, there was an affluence of life, and certainty of flow, such as excited my wonder, while it baffled my comprehension. I could talk a while when the evening commenced: but the first gush of vivacity and fluency gone, I was fain to sit on a stool at Diana's feet, to rest my head on her knee, and listen alternately to her and Mary; while they sounded thoroughly the topic on which I had but touched. Diana offered to teach me German.... Our natures dovetailed: mutual affection—of the strongest kind—was the result.... Thus occupied, and mutually entertained, days passed like hours, and weeks like days. (447)

In this passage Jane describes being "in love," and with words like "handsome," "vigorous," "animal spirits," and "certainty of flow," Brontë appropriates masculine qualities for Diana. She speaks with a "certain authority," demonstrating how well masculine qualities become her and by extension might become other women. In spite of Diana's beauty and strength and Jane's strong attraction to her, the novel veers away from the suggestion of overt sapphism.

When Jane returns to Rochester, the focus shifts to his body, and almost nothing further is said of Jane's body. It becomes invisible. Jane returns strong, independent, with wealth and a family, and with the gaze appropriated as her own. She tells Rochester, "I am independent, sir, as well as rich: I am my own mistress," and these traditional patriarchal markers of male power comprise the first of several subversive repetitions Brontë performs while bringing the novel to a close (556). Jane finds Rochester's body violently disfigured, a body blind, maimed, and scarred. He is powerless and dependent. Rather than a slave in the Reed household, a schoolmistress at Lowood or Morton, rather than a dead body in India, Jane becomes Rochester's eyes and "right hand" (577).

Significantly, the text clearly states that it is Rochester's left hand that is missing (552), and yet, Jane becomes his "right hand."[44] Hands connote creation, work, and activity, with the right hand usually the stronger of the two. The textual shift from "left" to "right" symbolizes the extent of the exchange of power taking place. Jane is not at his right side; she *is* his eyes and right hand, assuming a position of primacy and control.

Rich writes that the quality which makes Brontë's heroines so valuable to women readers is their "determined refusal of the romantic."[45] The Thornfield section of *Jane Eyre*, although often referred to as if it were the entire novel, is one of four major parts. The erotic attraction and eventual union of Jane and Rochester—the classic romance plot—exists within the larger narrative of Jane's movement from the victimization of the Reed household to the agency of authoring her own story. While still within the binary heterosexual circle, Jane becomes "giver and protector," "prop and guide," with the vision and power to interpret their world.

After two years of total blindness, Rochester asks, "have you a glittering ornament round your neck?... And have you a pale blue dress on?" (577). By answering in the affirmative, by feeding his words back to him, Jane validates what he sees and shapes his new vision. In light of Shuttleworth's claim that power in Brontë's fiction resides with the figure who can read the other while preserving the illegibility of the self, Rochester's blindness takes on even more significance.[46] In the end Rochester just barely begins to regain his vision as Jane retrains his eyes to see through her mediation. Rather than being chained to a man—a possibility referred to earlier in relation to both Rochester and St. John—Jane now wears the gold watch-chain, and by isolating this couple at Ferndean, Brontë has put a stop to Jane's every-changing body as both consequence and object of another's gaze. Certainly not a conventional union, in this marriage of reversals Jane, with wealth and power, becomes the desiring subject.

While the old romance plot complete with a fairy-tale ending runs parallel to the subversion in *Jane Eyre*, in the end Jane does not merely desire marriage. If that were the case, she could have accepted St. John River's proposal. She desires marriage with her lover; they are married, and she gives birth to a son. Yet, the narrative does not close with the marriage and son as sign of Jane's sexual fulfillment, but concludes with the words of St. John Rivers. Perhaps this displaced emphasis on St. John screens *Jane Eyre*'s subversion, or perhaps it is a lapse on Brontë's part. Yet, it is possible to read it differently.

Given Jane's rebellion as a young child, given her ability to learn control as well as French and music at Lowood that, in turn, enabled her to move on, and given her feelings of dissatisfaction at Thornfield, another possible reading of this ending emerges. On the high roof of Thornfield looking over field and hill, Jane "longed for a power of vision which might overpass the limit; which might reach the busy world, towns, regions full of life" (132). She never achieves this kind of vision, and along with her happiness in Rochester, she still possesses this desire to "overpass the limits" of her historical time and her particular biographic and geographic placement in that time. She ends with St. John Rivers because she envies his liberty to assert his ambition and pursue his quest. The desire to overpass limits sounds a constant refrain in *Jane Eyre,* and because Brontë ends with this refrain rather than the marriage or the birth of the son, it intrudes upon and detracts from those events.

Overall, happy marriages do not abound in *Jane Eyre.* Mrs. Reed is a widow and Mrs. Brocklehurst appears like a store-window mannequin advertising her husband's election. Maria Temple leaves Lowood to marry, but like the marriages of Diana and Mary Rivers, her marriage and her husband remain outside the narrative frame. Rochester's marriage to Bertha Mason is an exploitive, abusive, and dehumanizing affair. The projected marriage between Rochester and Blanche Ingram would be a mere legal contract for the sake of property and rank. Rosamond Oliver is madly in love with St. John, and although passionately attracted to her, he refuses to marry her, telling Jane, "while I love Rosamond Oliver so wildly...I experience at the same time a calm, unwarped consciousness...that to twelve months' rapture would succeed a lifetime of regret. This I know" (476–77). St. John does want Jane as a wife because she can be the "sufferer," "labourer," and "female apostle" he desires, but Jane does not want to play "female apostle" to St. John as Christ. Finally, Jane and Rochester marry, but Brontë has to isolate them at Ferndean and go to great lengths in terms of her wealth and his disfigurement to equalize the relationship. Even though Jane can satisfy her sexual desire in the end, this narrative is not about happy marriages. Rather, it is a detailed analysis and commentary on the near impossibility of satisfying female desire in a patriarchal world rife with men like John Reed, Rev. Brocklehurst, Edward Rochester, and St. John Rivers.

Lucy Snowe and the Politics of Location

> *I sometimes wonder if you expect me to return calls and repay civilities like a Christian or whether it is sufficiently understood between us that I am a heathen and an outlaw.*
>
> George Eliot
> *Letters*, June 1853

Near-sighted, small and plain, Charlotte Brontë lived physically and geographically marginalized, a woman without social standing, wealth or beauty, isolated in northern England. However, a politics of location emerged at the intersection of Brontë's marginalization and her rich and full experiences with language, a politics of location that repeats itself in her last complete novel, *Villette*, published in 1853. Small, plain and poor, Lucy Snowe also secures agency through marginalization in combination with reading and writing. This chapter investigates the connection between location and interpretation in *Villette*, focusing on Lucy's skills as a reader, the novel's implied readers, and a number of critical responses.

A continually self-reflexive text, *Villette* is all about reading. The different texts Lucy reads include other characters, works of art, theater performances, the domestic romance enacted by John Bretton and Paulina Home, and the Gothic romance enacted by Ginevra Fanshawe and the Count de Hamel. Lucy is as concerned with her reading as she is with her personal history, and through continual addresses to readers consisting of directions, advice, and warnings, she insists that they also be conscious of their participation in constructing the story.

When Lucy first appears, she is staying at her godmother's house in Bretton, already once removed from her first home and first mother, and this theme of homelessness repeats itself as she continues to move from place to place. Where is her home? Who is her father?

What has happened to her family? The questions are never answered, and any expectation that they eventually will be is frustrated. Lucy's very homelessness allows for new ways of seeing, estrangement and uncertainty enabling her to create a space for new perceptions and changing perspectives. In reading *Villette* as a critique and rejection of the center as oppressive and exploitive for women, in reading Lucy's continual displacement as a study in the politics of location, I read against an attitude toward "home" prevalent in much narrative before and after Brontë and against an abundance of criticism that discusses Lucy mainly in terms of morbidity, deprivation, and defeat.

Signifying a place rather than a heroine's name, *Villette* asks readers to think immediately in terms of location. The plot also encourages this attention to place, establishing one context only to abandon it for another, moving from place to place only to create a sense of the ultimate limitation of any one place. In the many different locations—Bretton, Miss Marchmont's, London, Villette, and within Villette the Rue Fossette, La Terrasse, the Hôtel Crécy, and the Faubourg Clotilde—Lucy repeats culturally intelligible roles— goddaughter, nurse, victim, governess, lover, actress, teacher—only to deconstruct these identities through caustic observation. In these various locations, characters who support and enable the dominant paradigm are analyzed and dismissed. Without family, father, wealth or beauty, Lucy, although in the system, is marginalized, and from the distance of her estrangement she can read her surroundings and criticize—sometimes bitterly, sometimes humorously.

Early in *Villette* Lucy offers a choice in unraveling her story, inviting the reader in the first paragraphs of Chapter IV to read the narrative subversively:

> It will be conjectured that I was of course glad to return to the bosom of my kindred. Well! the amiable conjecture does no harm, and may therefore be safely left uncontradicted. Far from saying nay, indeed, I will permit the reader to picture me, for the next eight years, as a bark slumbering through halcyon weather ....[1]

The irony and play heard in phrases like "bosom of my kindred" appears frequently in *Villette*, and, as Brenda R. Silver notes, "the irony of Lucy's 'permission' to her readers to deceive themselves emphasizes society's refusal to see or to admit the actual circumstances of her—and by implication other women's—existence."[2] After reading these paragraphs, one may be fairly certain that at this point any conjecture regarding Lucy's happiness constitutes a displaced reading. Another story is being told here, and a reader can, if he chooses, refuse the romantic ideal and begin to construct an ironic and intelligent character.

Thus, at least two implied readers emerge early in *Villette*: the conventional reader who accepts the cultural maxims about women in patriarchy and wants to find them mirrored in novels, and that other reader—that skeptical and rebellious reader in whom Lucy can confide. The meaning of *Villette* depends, then, on the reader's capacity to consider the interpretive activity in which she is engaged and her desire for something other than traditional romance. While writers like Walter Scott and George Eliot employ strategies that continually announce that a story is being told, Brontë replaces the idea of "a story" with multiple stories and deferred meaning. New information emerging throughout the narrative triggers new interpretations; mutually exclusive possibilities exist, and the narrator even offers a choice of endings.[3]

On the second page of the novel when Lucy's godmother, Mrs. Bretton, comes to fetch her, she "plainly saw events coming" and rescues Lucy from the "unsettled sadness." Lucy remembers her past as "a long time, of cold, of danger, of contention," but that is all we are told, and the narrative remains intentionally vague (1:39). Brontë leaves readers to imagine any number of awful possibilities—abuse, poverty, disease and death. In contrast, Mrs. Bretton's house appears handsome and pleasant with large peaceful rooms and "clear, wide windows," a place where time flows smoothly. Mrs. Bretton's son, John, the same age as Lucy, occupies center stage in his mother's life. Almost immediately Polly Home, a distant relation, arrives, and from the sidelines Lucy performs her first reading of character.

In spite of the periodic praise given to Polly Home, the text inserts a wedge between the reader and this petite, doll-like character. Rather than identification with Polly, this distance positions the reader with Lucy as spectator and critic. For example, at the age of six Polly insists on serving her father tea, and Lucy narrates:

> Throughout the meal she continued her attentions: rather absurd they were.
> The sugar-tongs were too wide for one of her hands, and she had to use both

in wielding them; the weight of the silver cream-ewer...tasked her insufficient
strength and dexterity, but she would lift this, hand that.... Candidly
speaking, I thought her a little busy-body. (1:14)

In addition to serving tea, Polly also hems a handkerchief as a
keepsake for her father "with a needle, that in her fingers seemed
almost a skewer, pricking herself ever and anon, marking the cambric
with a track of minute red dots; occasionally starting when the
perverse weapon—swerving from her control—inflicted a deeper stab
than usual; but still silent, diligent, absorbed, womanly" (1:15). Later
in the novel instead of making a keepsake for her father, Polly wears
a white dress "sprinkled slightly with drops of scarlet" (2:29). The
repetition of the color white sprinkled with red signifies that rather
than making it, Polly has become the keepsake and prize, ready for
marriage to John Bretton.

In several scenes Polly positions herself face down on the floor,
and it is difficult to imagine a more obsequious body position. When
John excludes Polly from his birthday party, Lucy attempts to
console her with "maxims of philosophy," but Polly stops her ears
with her fingers and lies on the mat "with her face against the flags;
nor could either Warren or the cook root her from that position"
(1:28). When John hears that Polly must leave, he hardly takes
notice, and she again prostrates her body on the floor:

"Little Mousie" crept to his side, and lay down on the carpet at his feet, her
face to the floor; mute and motionless she kept that post and position till bed-
time. Once I saw Graham [John]—wholly unconscious of her proximity—push
her with his restless foot. She receded an inch or two. A minute after one little
hand...softly caressed the heedless foot. (1:34)

Certainly, this type of narration exceeds mere storytelling. In all her
personal relations, Polly expresses no interests in women or desires
other than pleasing men, and the narrator's commentary is a harsh
satire and rejection of Polly's masochistic behavior.

After her initial appearance in the first chapters of Volume One,
Polly disappears until the first chapter of Volume Two. Almost a
decade has passed, and Lucy and (the now) Dr. John are at the theater.
Polly is also there with her father, clinging "very quietly and steadily"
to him, when the theater erupts in fire. During the panic Polly is

struck down onto the floor and "hurled under the feet of the crowd." Without recognizing her, Dr. John lifts her, asking, "She is very light...like a child!... Is she a child, Lucy? Did you notice her age?" (2:13). Although a young woman, Polly remains in need of masculine protection, and as this scene suggests, one man seems insufficient for the task.

Near the close of *Villette,* a "delicate, silky, loving, and loveable little doggie" appears at Mme. Beck's pensionnat, a little spaniel completely devoted to M. Paul. Lucy remarks, "I never saw her [the dog], but I thought of Paulina de Bassompierre: forgive the association, reader, it *would* occur" [original emphasis] (2:211). Although Lucy displays some affection toward Polly, the overall judgment is a dismissal of this androcentric kind of womanhood.[4] As Polly is passed from father to husband in marriage, we can see the alliance between the two men forming and solidifying. Polly symbolically plaits locks of her father's and Dr. John's hair together with her own: "she *tie*d it like a *knot*, *prison*ed it in a *lock*et, and laid it on her heart" [emphasis added] (2:237). This diction serves as a notable example of double-voiced discourse, signaling the narrator's censorious attitude in conversation with Polly's contentment. The courtship and marriage of Dr. John and Polly might well be the central plot and happy ending of another kind of novel, but in the framework of *Villette* this traditional romance proves unsatisfactory and reductive. Brontë subversively repeats it to display its inadequacy.

Again and again, *Villette* reveals the power of language to shape and determine experience and the importance of participating in this activity. Upon Lucy's arrival in London an explicit thematics of language use emerges where the distinction between Lucy as narrator and Lucy as character is a crucial one. The narrator has at her disposal a proficiency in English, French, and German, multiple cultural and political perspectives, and the knowledge and confidence that Lucy as character is in the process of acquiring. In London Lucy the character hears an English dialect so different, she can barely understand it. After crossing the channel, the difficulty intensifies when she arrives in Villette, where she becomes speechless: "I could say nothing whatever; not possessing a phrase of *speaking* French: and it was French, and French only, the whole world seemed now gabbling round me" (1:72).

Throughout the novel sentences and passages appear in French without translation, and thus, non-French speaking readers experience a similar frustration as Lucy. The incorporation of a second language in women's writing can function as a subversive gesture, and Patricia S. Yaeger writes that the "second language serves an emancipatory function...enacting a moment in which the novel's primary language is put into process, a moment of possible transformation when the writer forces her speech to break out of old representations of the feminine and to posit something new."[5] By the novel's end, Lucy has acquired fluency in French, and in addition to decorum and genre, she has learned to decenter her primary and secondary languages.

In contrast to her developing language skills, Lucy's unchanging physical appearance hardly signifies power. Yet, frequently and in interesting and sometimes subtle ways, she uses her small body to control a situation. When Polly, moaning and complaining of heartache, despairs over the departure of her papa, Lucy says, "I roused myself and started up, to check this scene while it was yet within bounds" (1:8). Surrounded by watermen at the London wharf, Lucy does nothing when one of the men places his hands on her trunk, "I looked on and waited quietly; but when another laid hands on me, I spoke up, shook off his touch, stepped at once into a boat, desired austerely that the trunk should be placed beside me—'Just there'" (1:58). When Ginevra is seasick, Lucy again asserts this authority: "Indignant at last with her teazing peevishness, I curtly requested her 'to hold her tongue.' The rebuff did her good, and it was observable that she likes me no worse for it" (1:67). Often Lucy speaks to Ginevra in this way, explaining that "a salutary setting down always agreed with her" (1:103). Upon first arriving in Villette, Lucy aggressively asks a stranger for help (1:73). At the Rue Fossette, Mme. Beck questions her and tells her to return in the morning, but Lucy counters, "it will be better that I should stay here this night" (1:78). Rather than being powerless, Lucy engages in an economical use of energy and power, all the more effective because so at variance with conventional expectations.

When Mme. Beck asks Lucy to substitute teach for the English master in the second division class, Lucy's determination equals the task. Although she has never taught before, she enters a class of sixty students—"rondes, franches, brusques, et tant soit peu rebelles" who "always throw over timid teachers" (1:95). In the midst of the "wild herd" and its insolent and noisy campaign to overthrow her, she does two things. First, she reads the composition of the "most vicious" student before the class, and every student is silenced but one, who stands shouting next to a closet door. Second, she calmly pushes this student into the closet and locks the door. Her ability to act aggressively in this initial teaching situation pays off, resulting in her promotion from bonne d'enfants to English teacher.

Before traveling to Villette, Lucy had lived in "two hot, close rooms" as nurse and companion to Miss Marchmont. About her promotion to English teacher Lucy says, "Yes...I am a rising character: once an old lady's companion, then a nursery-governess, now a school-teacher" (1:74). Impressed by such mobility, Ginevra says, "I wonder you are not more flattered by all this...you take it with strange composure. If you really are the nobody I once thought you, you must be a cool hand" (2:72). Although often read as timid, reticent, and passive, Lucy performs differently when there is something to be accomplished, displaying a quickness and audacity that subvert the image of the passive female. A "cool hand," she takes advantage of every opportunity; still, she can say about her promotion to English teacher, "Madame raised my salary; but she got thrice the work out of me she had extracted from Mr Wilson, at half the expense" (1:98). She asserts her success only to balance it with an awareness of the exploitation embedded in the promotion. Readers may assume the promotion is good only to have Lucy qualify and read it differently.

During another self-conscious moment, Lucy comments on her own appearance, explaining how her staid manner operates as a cloak and hood, "since under its favour I had been enabled to achieve with impunity, and even approbation, deeds that if attempted with an excited and unsettled air, would in some minds have stamped me as a dreamer and zealot" (1:50). Her staid manner both conceals and generates all kinds of abnormal behavior: voyaging from rural England to London and then Villette, desiring two men rather than the customary one "true love," dressing and playing the part of a man in the school play, wandering through Villette at night in a drug-altered state, and, finally, not marrying anyone but creating a positive place of solitude where she becomes financially independent, a proficient user of French, a teacher of English, and an author.

At the Musée des Beaux Arts, Lucy performs another reading, entertaining her audience with a description of Rubens's *Cleopatra* and a set of four paintings entitled *La vie d'une femme* (1:254). Lucy reacts, "What women to live with! insincere, ill-humored, bloodless, brainless nonentities! As bad in their way as the indolent gipsy-giantess, the Cleopatra, in hers" (1:255). Nevertheless, the paintings represent the possibilities of womanhood—whore, virgin, wife, and mother—as M. Paul and Dr. John comprehend it. We see these static and lifeless representations of womanhood framed and encased in the museum, but outside the museum, fixed gender roles come undone, never stay in one place, constantly shift and slip as gender trouble persists in *Villette*.

Brontë toys with body size and performance in the frequent comparisons of Mme. Beck to a man, in the petite bodies of Polly Home and M. Paul, in the petite and pretty appearance and small hands and feet of Count de Hamel, in Mme. Walravens's beard and male voice, in Lucy's performance as a fop in the school play, and in the appearances of the transvestite nun. Patricia E. Johnson writes that both sides of any axis that can be constructed—private/public, love/work, male/female—are problematic for women: choosing either side means immediate confinement within a system that deforms women to patriarchal ends.[6] Critics often accuse Lucy of neurosis and duplicity because she refuses to choose or she cannot make a choice. However, as Johnson notes, in her movement between the two sides, Lucy finds her own voice, and to see such oscillation as sickness or compromise is to ignore its creative aspect.[7] Not only are "female" and "woman" relational terms changing in relation to context, but Lucy's changes exceed the binary of female/male as she appears as multiple subjects in the alleé defendue, attic, schoolroom, and drawing room, as spectator at the theater and performer on the stage. She is not simply a "man" or a "woman" or a mixture of the two. The continual re-signification of "Lucy Snowe" exceeds any simple binary, refusing any stable notion of identity and fiercely resisting domestication.

Lucy overcomes barriers of gender and size in her gradual but certain ascent from nurse in the closed and humid space of Miss Marchmont's sickroom to governess to teacher. Unlike Dr. John and the others, M. Paul can read more of Lucy's character—her passion, desire and ambition—and Lucy accepts his help. Yet, while M. Paul helps Lucy, it is important to note that the initial idea of founding a school is her own. She paces the alley thinking, "how I should make some advance in life, take another step towards an independent position...little by little, I had laid half a plan" (2:139). Lucy tells M. Paul her plan, and, significantly, he asks her to tell it and retell it (2:244). This repetition in language is crucial to instituting the plan, making it seem plausible and bringing it into the realm of possibility.

In spite of his intelligence and the affection that grows between Lucy and M. Paul, *Villette*'s power to subvert and transform conventional plots demands that he die. M. Paul will hinder Lucy's development. He *will* censor her novels, and he will continue to believe in the ideal passive female (2:121, 131). Perhaps the most revealing incident regarding M. Paul's character occurs just after he has told a story. Although his powers of oral storytelling are impressive, he explains that he could not write out his stories: "I hate the mechanical labour. I hate to stoop and sit still. I could dictate it, though, with pleasure to an amanuensis who suited me. Would Mademoiselle Lucy write for me if I asked her?" (2:165). He continues in this vein, "Try some day; let us see the monster I can make of myself under the circumstances. But just now, there is no question of dictation; I mean to make you useful in another office" (2:165–66). M. Paul has to die, then, because he can only see Lucy in a subordinate position, supporting and expanding his sense of worth and confidence and transcribing his language rather than creating her own.

In his beliefs and lifestyle, M. Paul is often compared to a Jesuit priest, and his father confessor and mentor is Pére Silas. At one point in the narrative, Lucy explains why she cannot visit Pére Silas, and, by analogy, this explanation works well to clarify the need for M. Paul's death:

> Did I, do you suppose, reader, contemplate venturing again within that worthy priest's reach? As soon should I have thought of walking into a Babylonish furnace.... [T]he probabilities are that had I visited Numero 10, Rue des Mages, at the hour and day appointed, I might just now, instead of writing this heretic narrative, be counting my beads in the cell of a certain Carmelite convent.... [W]hatever I may think of his Church and creed (and I like neither), of himself I must ever retain a grateful recollection. He was kind when I needed kindness; he did me good. (1:205)

Lucy welcomes the friendship, affection, and help offered by Père Silas and M. Paul before his departure. They sustain her. Nevertheless, as Janet Freeman notes, "The storm that may or may not have caused M. Paul's death on his way home marks the end of *Villette,* but it is not the end of Lucy Snowe's life."[8] Her life continues, and rather than counting beads or serving as M. Paul's secretary, Lucy is able to fashion her own story. Three decisive aspects of *Villette*'s ending make it a radical closure and reaffirm the novel as a "heretic narrative." First, the narrative ends in the heroine's solitude and vocation rather than in her marriage or death. Second, Lucy writes in the last chapter, "M. Emanuel was away three years. Reader, they were the three happiest years of my life. Do you scout the paradox?" (2:309). These three years were years with the idea of love but not its day-to-day experience, without the physical intimacy but also without the stress, subordination and confinement that would come with marriage to M. Paul. Third, we know that Lucy goes on to author this text, and so, *Villette* becomes a writing beyond the ending. Had M. Paul returned, the story of *Villette* could not have been told or would be told from a different perspective: Lucy as storyteller would not be born. As in *Jane Eyre,* this unique and disruptive first-person narrator creates the subversion, and the telling of the story—along with its grief and sadness—becomes the pay-off.

Rachel Blau DuPlessis defines "writing beyond the ending" as the "invention of strategies that sever the narrative from formerly conventional structures of fiction and consciousness about women."[9] In constructing her story of women writers as a story of origins wherein postromantic strategies begin at a particular historical moment, DuPlessis argues that in 1883 with the publication of *The Story of an African Farm* Olive Schreiner "breaks the sentence." Such a break allows alternative and oppositional stories to be created beyond the teleological formulations of quest and romance. DuPlessis states that Schreiner's novel is a critique of dominant narratives, "a critique deliberately articulated, intellectually principled, and emotionally coherent."[10] Although the phrase "emotionally coherent" may not suit the complexity of Lucy as narrator and Lucy as character, *Villette* performs a deliberate and principled critique of the domestic romance represented by Polly and Dr. John and the Gothic romance represented by Ginevra and de Hamel. Lucy Snowe inherits but is alienated from these types of traditional romance because she has no wealth, social standing, or family and, as DuPlessis notes, her body is "incompletely formed" for them. Both Lucy's body and her social and economic "mis-fortune" provide a distance and tone with which she can read the sentimental and Gothic narratives internal to the plot.

According to DuPlessis, the choice of the teller or perspective will alter the narrative's core assumptions.[11] One need only imagine *Villette* told from Mme. Beck's or Dr. John's point of view to understand the subversion operating in Lucy's first person narration. Lucy remains outside the conventional romantic frame, allowing for the telling and interpretation of the dramas internal to *Villette*'s larger structure. Much of *Villette* functions as witty and pointed satire of a dominant social formation where women—Mrs. Bretton, Ginevra, Polly—engage in parasitic relations with men. The satire means to provoke an anti-mimetic response in the implied reader. To miss the multiplicity of narrative levels and the oppositional project present in *Villette* is to erase the agency and reduce the narrative to melodrama.[12]

Lucy consistently views Ginevra with a bemused disdain, and along with the reader Lucy develops a realization of Dr. John's and M. Paul's limitations. Yet, DuPlessis, in her brief reading of *Villette*, writes that Lucy "yearns for traditional feminine destinies of protection and Home," and in the end Lucy "is denied the unprecedented resolution of marriage and vocation.... Here too independence and quest have been punished with deprivation of love."[13] What Lucy is "deprived" of is marriage with M. Paul, and it seems especially odd in the context of DuPlessis's discussion that a refusal of this kind of marriage would be called "deprivation." Later in her discussion, DuPlessis comments that "Love, along with domesticity and beauty, is the third term creating the traditional boundaries that mold and define women."[14] What definition of "love" is operating in these two quotations? To be punished by the deprivation of "love" would mean "love" is a thing to be desired. However, if love constitutes the third term creating traditional boundaries that mold and define women, "love" would be undesirable. While DuPlessis's use of the word "love" appears problematic, in terms of "love," "domesticity," and "beauty," Brontë remained inflexible in her decision to withhold these decoys from Lucy and to end the novel with her solitude, strength, and professional standing.

About *Villette*'s ending, Brontë told Gaskell that Mr. Brontë disliked novels which left a melancholy impression. He asked his daughter to make the hero and heroine, like the heroes and heroines in fairy-tales, marry and live happily ever after. However, the idea of Paul's death assumed the force of reality in Brontë's mind, and all she could do in compliance with her father's wish was to veil the fate in oracular words, leaving it to the character and discernment of her readers to interpret her meaning.[15] By enclosing the domestic and Gothic fairy tales within a larger narrative, Brontë acknowledges their presence and effect but, more importantly, she reduces them to parts of the whole, to some possible outcomes. Through this complex manipulation of narrative framing, Brontë creates a new space for women outside the circle of traditional romance and marriage.

Referring to Lucy as "a kind of fly-on-the-wall focalizer gaining access of vision by virtue of her insignificance," Karen Lawrence writes that "Lucy's plainness allows her to reverse the gaze.... Lucy Snowe avoids the fate of spectacle and becomes spectator instead."[16] The different ways DuPlessis and Lawrence read Lucy represent significant differences in interpretation existing since the time of *Villette*'s publication. While examining some of this criticism, it is helpful to keep in mind Lucy's explicit invitations to readers to read differently.

At the time of *Villette*'s publication, Harriet Martineau and Brontë were good friends. In 1850 Brontë had visited Martineau for a week and told a friend that she relished Martineau's company inexpressibly. In 1853 Martineau reviewed *Villette* for the London *Daily News*, and while many aspects of Martineau's own life seem unconventional, she interpreted the novel through a conventional filter. She refused the novel's explicit invitation to read subversively beyond the traditional story of romantic love and marriage, writing instead: "All the female characters, in all their thoughts and lives, are full of one thing, or are regarded by the reader in the light of that one thought—love."[17] Had Martineau pursued the implication of her statement "or are regarded by the reader in the light of that one thought," she might have arrived at other conclusions about *Villette*. Brontë's irritation with Martineau's review was so great that their friendship came to an abrupt end.

Like Martineau, Gilbert and Gubar read Lucy Snowe through the ideology of romantic love, writing that Lucy is "from first to last a woman *without*—outside society, without parents or friends, without physical or mental attractions, without money or confidence or health."[18] Yet, Lucy does possess strength, determination, and intelligence, and these characteristics help her to make the long voyage from Bretton to Miss Marchmont's to London to the Rue Fossette and, finally, to her own establishment in the Faubourg Clotilde as mistress. The long voyage ends in security, independence and health, what Nancy Sorkin Rabinowitz calls "a new kind of solitude, one that is founded on proprietorship and work."[19] To include "society" and Lucy's lack of physical beauty in their list gives an importance to social status and beauty that Brontë undermines in *Villette* as well as in *Jane Eyre*. By reading *Villette* as "perhaps the most moving and terrifying account of female deprivation ever written," Gilbert and Gubar erase the other vital aspects Brontë strategically forces into this story, other positive places for women traditionally obscured by the very parents, society, beauty, and wealth that Gilbert and Gubar would elegize.

In the novel, Dr. John is a man centrally located with wealth, beauty, confidence, health, family and friends, but he is a bad reader. He falls madly in love with the shallow Ginevra Fanshawe; he judges the actress Vashti as a woman rather than an artist, and often he simply fails to recognize Lucy at all. Lucy says of him: "With now welcome force, I realized his entire misapprehension of my character and nature. He wanted always to give me a role not mine. Nature and I opposed him. He did not at all guess what I felt: he did not read my eyes, or face, or gestures; though, I doubt not, all spoke" (2:85). Nevertheless, at one point in their discussion, Gilbert and Gubar align themselves with Dr. John by writing, "Dr. John is correct, then, in assuming that the nun comes out of Lucy's diseased brain."[20] In describing Lucy as "from first to last a woman *without*" and by italicizing the "*without*," Gilbert and Gubar disclose their unwillingness to read Lucy's character as a subversive repetition of womanhood with a difference. Lucy's "homelessness" accentuates the androcentric configurations of womanhood represented so persuasively in female characters like Polly Home and Ginevra Fanshawe. In a different country, in a different language, in a different body, and often in an "unfeminine" voice of sarcasm, irony, and comic mockery, Lucy reveals a great deal about the pain and power of female autonomy.

Villette, as Linda C. Hunter claims, may be the first English novel to deal with the heroine's work as an integral part of her life.[21] After Paul's death, the school continues to prosper and Lucy, by the time she writes her narrative, knows the West End of London as well as her beloved city. Silver writes that Lucy "has survived the destruction of the romantic fantasy and grown into another reality." Brontë moves the narrative frame and the heroine completely out of heterosexist coupling and into autonomy, work, and success, a situation Silver refers to as intellectually, financially and existentially fulfilling.[22]

The appearance of the ghostly nun in *Villette* garners a fair amount of critical attention, but, overall, the interpretations are too solemn, missing the whole sense of play and satire in the figure. This very Catholic image of womanhood is a ruse, a practical joke. The ghost's appearance is well known to everyone at the pensionnat, and many believe the nun to be the ghost of a woman buried alive for breaking her vows. However, rather than fearing the ghost, each time she appears, Lucy becomes bolder, and on the nun's third appearance, Lucy asks, "Who are you? and why do you come to me?" Lucy advances: "I stretched out my hand, for I meant to touch her. She seemed to recede. I drew nearer: her recession, still silent, became swift" (2:58–59).

Dr. John believes that the sightings are due entirely to "Lucy's diseased brain." But in the last pages of the novel Lucy and readers discover that this ghostly nun is a costume covering the body of Count Alfred de Hamel, Ginevra's lover, who uses the affect of "the nun" as a smoke screen. This facade makes possible their secret trysts in the midst of Madame Beck's intense surveillance, and on the night they elope, they leave the nun's costume on Lucy's bed. To take a solemn approach to the nun misses the joke. Kate Millett calls *Villette* one of the wittier novels in English, and states that criticism of the Brontës

> has been a long game of masculine prejudice wherein the player either proves they can't write and are hopeless primitives, whereupon the critic sets himself up like a schoolmaster [like M. Paul] to edit their stuff and point out where they went wrong, or converts them into case histories from the wilds, occasionally prefacing his moves with a few pseudo-sympathetic remarks about the windy house on the moors, or old maidenhood, following with an

attack on every truth the novels contain, waged by anxious pedants who fear Charlotte might "castrate" them or Emily "unman" them with her passion.[23]

Replacing a belief in ghosts with a belief in the unconscious, other critical interpretations of the nun insist on psychoanalytic readings. The ghostly nun will be Lucy's double, the correlative of Lucy's neurotic inner self, and a symbol of repressed sexual desires. Christina Crosby performs a Lacanian reading of the nun only to question its suitability in her concluding paragraphs, writing, "To read the text as simply narcissistic, a symptom of Brontë's improper assimilation of the law of the Father, is to depend once again on the phallus...which is always discovered behind the veil, in sharp contrast to the indeterminacy of *Villette*'s revelations."[24] In Brontë's words, nothing remains when Lucy tears the veil—"all the movement was mine, so was all the life, the reality, the substance, the force" (2:282). One of Brontë's major points here is that viewer and context—the location—determine what is seen.

In *Villette* the voices populating language are organized into a structured stylistic system expressing the socio-ideological position of the author amid the heteroglossia of her epoch. Brontë is not speaking in the languages of major characters like M. Paul or Dr. John, but through their languages to orchestrate her own intentions, to build a superstructure over these languages made of her intentions and accents.[25] Moreover, what makes *Villette* an especially rich narrative is the intersection and friction between the social languages of French and English. The novel represents, analyzes, and evaluates the actions and consequences of multiple and diverse points of view. While conventional characters like Mme. Beck and Mrs. Bretton speak with authority and persuasion, it is the first-person narrator, her constant displacement, her relationship with readers, and the radical ending which combine to form an over-arching pattern of disruption and subversion.

Two passages in *Villette* function as reminders of the dialogic elements that saturate the text and the larger discursive world. When the other teachers and students leave the pensionnat during the vacation, Lucy, complaining about the loneliness, addresses her various readers, "religious reader," "moralist," "stern sage," "stoic," "cynic," and "epicure," realizing they will respond in various ways— with a sermon, frown, sneer or laugh (1:197). Although she knows that readers approach and interpret her character from different perspectives, the narrator thinks that if put in her situation, they might react in similar ways.

She also realizes that characters within the narrative frame interpret "Lucy" in diverse ways:

> What contradictory attributes of character we sometimes find ascribed to us, according to the eye with which we are viewed! Madame Beck esteemed me learned and blue; Miss Fanshawe, caustic, ironic, and cynical; Mr Home, a model teacher, the essence of the sedate and discreet: somewhat conventional perhaps, too strict, limited and scrupulous, but still the pink and pattern of governess-correctness; whilst another person, Professor Paul Emanuel, to wit, never lost an opportunity of intimating his opinion that mine was rather a fiery and rash nature—adventurous, indocile, and audacious. (2:64)

The word "Lucy" means all these things. Rather than negate or contradict the multiplicity, the text embraces it. The constant instability and slippage acknowledged in *Villette* challenges readers, even pardoning them if they must read conventionally.

In her biography, Gaskell relates how each night after family prayers and after everyone else had gone to bed, the three Brontë sisters paced "up and down (like restless wild animals) in the parlour, talking over plans and projects, and thoughts of what was to be their future life."[26] Charlotte and her sisters shared two dreams, to become writers and to own their own school. Lucy achieves both dreams.

Still, in the midst of Lucy's success, a core identity does not emanate from her character; different characters react differently to her, and critics read her differently. The ruptures, disturbances and ambiguity form the very source and substance of *Villette*'s power. In the midst of a vertical and horizontal array of values, beliefs and philosophies, Lucy and the text adamantly refuse to clear the air of confusion—to define Lucy Snowe's identity. Although no one can entirely escape the regulatory system, Lucy resists repeating "woman" within the bounds of a masculinist economy—that narrative performance belongs to female characters like Polly, Mrs. Bretton, Miss Marchmont, and Ginevra. Ginevra's questions "Who *are* you, Miss Snowe?" and "But *are* you anybody?" are answered in terms of action rather than identity. Marginality as a political location is much more than deprivation. In writing the story from the margins of her resistance, Lucy rewrites herself as the speaking subject who subverts a humanist identity, emphasizing instead process and performance. The traditionally dominant figures—Dr. John, Ginevra, and Polly— become the text, the objects of her talk and subjects of her reading. Lucy's ability to write her story represents her victory over the center. She records the painful struggles to celebrate the ending. Rather than repetitions constrained by the injunction to reconsolidate the old endings and naturalized identities, the differences in Lucy's performance of language constitute agency, bringing her culturally impossible life into the light.

Virginia Woolf In Her Father's Library

> *Then I have read a good deal, of many things,*
> *and reading makes me intensely happy, and*
> *culminates in a fit of writing always.*
>
> Virginia Woolf
> *Letters*, January 1905

> *She was a close and observant analyst of the*
> *world she lived in. And she was one of the*
> *century's most insatiable readers.*
>
> Hermione Lee
> *Virginia Woolf*

Virginia Woolf may appear, at first glance, to have little in common with Charlotte Brontë and George Eliot. Woolf was born in 1882, two years after Eliot's death, into an upper middle-class Victorian family and a large house with servants, located at 22 Hyde Park Gate, London. Certainly, Leslie Stephen's library would have been much larger than those of Patrick Brontë or Robert Evans, and in terms of geography, class, and beauty, Woolf was centrally located. Characterized as a member of the aristocratic and intellectual elite, Woolf was a member of Bloomsbury, and along with Gertrude Stein, Pound, T. S. Eliot, and Joyce, she gave rise to the Modernist Movement.

In her article on the perils of popularity, Brenda R. Silver analyzes Woolf as an icon whose prestige has risen in the world of high culture as well as the popular realm. From her 1937 appearance on the cover of *Time* and her 1970s feminist reconstruction as the "mother of us all" to her 1991 appearance at the top of the list of "What's In" in the MLA, there has been an ongoing and complex struggle over the signification of "Virginia Woolf." Silver writes that this popularity and prestige often occur without reference to her writing, and such success "can transform subversiveness into respectability."[1] Rather than respectability or popularity, however, this chapter focuses on the genesis of Woolf's subversiveness, beginning in the second half of the nineteenth century—the flip side of Silver's series of twentieth-century historical moments.

Woolf, like Brontë and Eliot, had brothers who enjoyed all the privileges of being sons in Victorian England, and like Brontë and Eliot, Woolf felt the sting of being raised as a "girl." In her teens she took lessons in Greek and Latin—the extent of her formal education—and, thus, Woolf had far less formal education than either Brontë or Eliot. She had to deal with many of the same pressures to marry and give birth, and along with her sister Vanessa, she was expected to serve the tea. She was a survivor of incest and experienced mental breakdown before publishing her first novel. She was frequently around doctors: they were in her house daily during the illness and death of her mother, her half-sister Stella, and her brother Thoby and during her father's long terminal illness. She was subjected to the Weir-Mitchell rest cure on four occasions.[2] In 1904 she wrote to Violet Dickinson, "I cant conceive how anybody can be fool enough to believe in a doctor.... My life is a constant fight against Doctors follies, it seems to me."[3] Hermione Lee writes that there is "no doubt that the development of her political position, her intellectual resistance to tyranny and conventionality, derived to a great extent from her experiences as a woman patient."[4]

In examining the factors and steps leading to Woolf's subversive writing, this chapter considers "Woolf" as a discursive site of intersection where nineteenth-century medical discourse, the Victorian family, and her father's library collide. In order to understand the importance of the library, it is necessary to understand the state of late nineteenth-century medicine and the family dynamics of the Stephen household. Thus, the chapter begins with an examination of nineteenth-century medical discourse to provide a sense of the dominant medical attitude toward women's health, education, and work at the time Woolf was born.

The branch of medical science called "gynaecology" emerged in the 1840s and was founded on the assumptions that women are closer to nature, reproductive in purpose, physically weaker and mentally inferior to men; women, as ministering angels and rewards, need no education beyond what will prepare them for reproduction and domesticity. Rather than education, they should commit themselves to service and duty, and their subordination is the will of God. In explaining the need for such assumptions, Charles E. Rosenberg writes that at least since the time of Hippocrates and Aristotle, women's subordinate roles have necessitated an elaborate body of medical justification, and this was especially true in the nineteenth century.[5]

Three physiological concepts—limited energy, sympathies of the womb, and acquired characteristics—were essential in constructing and maintaining this nineteenth-century view of women. The concept of limited energy imagined the body as a closed system with only a limited amount of energy; thus, the brain and ovaries could not develop at the same time. A woman's complex and delicate reproductive system developed and was put into good working order between the ages of fifteen and twenty-five, demanding all the body's energy, and as a result, a woman should not divert energy away from this important process in order to study or work outside the home.

The concept of sympathies referred to the sympathetic relation of the womb with all other parts of the body where shocks and irritation to the womb could cause disease in parts seemingly remote. Moreover, the uterus was connected to the central nervous system and any imbalances and shocks to the nervous system might cause pathological reactions and alter the reproductive cycle. This intimate hypothetical link between ovaries, uterus, and nervous system was the logical basis for the "reflex irritation" model of disease causation so popular in nineteenth-century medical textbooks. It was assumed by many nineteenth-century doctors that acquired physical and mental characteristics—acquired in one lifetime, that is—in the form of damage from disease and improper lifestyles would be transmitted through heredity. A woman's inappropriate behavior would not only affect her, but would result in the degeneration of the race as well. These three concepts comprised powerful tools in confining women to the home and denying them access to education and professional careers.

Many nineteenth-century doctors schooled in this sexist era accepted these three concepts as scientific truth, and they perceived and treated women accordingly. The American writer and physician S. Weir Mitchell is one such doctor.[6] In the 1870s Mitchell introduced his "rest cure," a treatment for neurasthenia and hysteria involving a specified period of seclusion, bed rest, massage, electrical muscular excitation, and over-feeding. The cure also included "moral medication" or psychotherapy that entailed conversations between the doctor and patient. As Ehrenreich and English observe, the cure was dependent on the now-familiar techniques of twentieth-century brainwashing—total isolation and sensory deprivation.[7] The patient was to lie on her back in a dimly lit room for six to eight weeks, was not permitted to read or write, and could have no visitors, seeing only the nurse and doctor. In severe cases she was forbidden to move independently, and even to turn over or rise to urinate, without assistance. Although Mitchell wrote that in some cases he "cured without fattening," the amount of food usually given during the cure was remarkable. Within ten days the patient was allowed three full meals daily along with three or four pints of milk. Within ten days two ounces of fluid malt extract were given before each meal, and large quantities of butter were served with every meal. The patient ate more by being fed by her attendant, and at the close of the first week Mitchell added one pound of beef daily in the form of raw soup.

While ostensibly a treatment of the body, the doctor's highest duty was altering the patient's "moral atmosphere," and Mitchell wrote that the "moral uses of enforced rest are readily estimated."[8] In describing one case study, he wrote, "I had won her full trust, and she obeyed, or tried to obey me, like a child," and this "childlike acquiescence in every needed measure" was essential for success.[9] Rather than independence, Mitchell worked to instill passivity, acceptance, obedience, and self-sacrifice in his patients. From his point of view women lived to serve their husbands and reproduce; they belonged at home where in their sweetness and simplicity, they nurtured children and cherished and accommodated husbands. His goal was to send the woman "home changed no less morally than physically," so that she will resume "her place in the family circle and in social life, a healthy and well-cured woman."[10] He wrote that careers "inevitably lessen her true attractiveness, and to my mind make her less fit to be the 'friendly lover and the loving friend'.... For most men, when she seizes the apple, she drops the rose."[11] Many of Mitchell's patients were, no doubt, struggling against this very ideal, this definition of womanhood; ironically Mitchell, confusing science and social policy, fought to restore them to domestication.

However inappropriate Mitchell's ideas may appear, several of his contemporaries expressed much harsher attitudes toward women's proper place and education. Dr. Withers Moore, senior physician to the Sussex County Hospital, Brighton, delivered the 1886 President's Address for the annual meeting of the British Medical Association. In his address, subsequently published in *The British Medical Journal* and entitled "The Higher Education of Women," Moore explained why women should not be trained and admitted to compete with men. He based his response on the part that "the mother has in making of the man—in determining, that is, the progress of the race." The training of women can only indispose and incapacitate them for their "proper function," the part that "Nature has assigned to them in the maintenance and progressive improvement of the human race. For bettering the breed of men, we need and claim to have the best *mothers of men*" [original emphasis]. Going back to the matter, the material itself, Moore wrote that the word "material" is Latin for mothering, "a lengthened out form of *mater*. We have no corresponding *paterial*." In Moore's narrative there are three characters—sons, men, and mothers, and "women are meant to be not men, but the mothers of men."[12]

In the same year, 1886, Dr. Willoughby Francis Wade delivered an Ingleby Lecture at Queen's College, Birmingham on "Some Functional Disorders of Females," subsequently published in the *British Medical Journal*. Wade was chairman of the British Medical Association's Scientific Grants Committee, and it was on his recommendation that research scholarships were endowed by the Association. He began the lecture by suggesting that the reproductive organs constituted the "central point of the human race, that round which all revolves, from which all radiates." Wade's female body was a passive body, a delicate vessel, where feelings were dominant. Woman's periodicity was conducive to the development of certain disorders, disorders which "are seated deep down in woman's nature and constitution, and therefore the tendency to them is never eradicated." Wade wrote that the "hope of marriage...is never quite extinguished in the female breast." When disappointed, effects differ: "if it takes a good woman to make a good wife, it takes a still better to make a good 'old maid.'" The instinctive business of a woman's life is the "attraction and retention of an admirer, the detection and annihilation of a rival."[13]

In 1905 in a similar vein, the eugenics theorist Dr. T. B. Hyslop lectured on occupation and environment as causative factors of insanity, a lecture also published in *The British Medical Journal*. A part of Hyslop's lecture merits quoting at length:

> We grant her the right of being a great civilizing agent as well as an ornament, but, intending woman to be mother, Nature fashioned her destiny for her. The departure of woman from her natural sphere to an artificial one involves a brain struggle which is deleterious to the virility of the race.... [G]irls are handicapped by considerations which ought to make them realize the futility of forcing education and undertaking work which only too frequently renders them neurotic and sexually incompetent. When we look the facts in the face and note the divergence of our women from the life-rôle entrusted to them by Nature, are we inspired with confidence as to the results for future generations? It is true that the more our women aspire to exercising their nervous and mental functions so they become not only less virile, but also less capable of generating healthy stock. Now not only is this a question concerning the virility of the race, but it has very direct bearings upon the increase of our nervous instability. In fact, the higher women strive to hold the torch of intellect, the dimmer the rays of light for the vision of their progeny.[14]

Hyslop was a powerful man, superintendent at Bethlem Royal Hospital, a prolific author, and a prominent lecturer and public speaker, and his power and influence were widespread. In direct opposition to the legal, social and medical changes that were taking place, Hyslop reiterated with no difference the nineteenth-century medical view toward women.

Rather than the exception, Mitchell, Moore, Wade, and Hyslop represent the dominant nineteenth-century medical view toward women. While some women were demanding equal pay for equal work, equal education, birth control, abortion, and sexual autonomy within marriage, a great number of doctors objected on moral grounds but registered their hostile reactions in and through medical discourse, using science to define and control female bodies. In seeking ways to maintain and recontextualize itself, patriarchy exploited physiology and the authority and power vested in medicine. These representative nineteenth-century doctors moved from the environment to internal physiological reactions, from circumstance to fact. Working deductively, their methodology was founded on preconceived assumptions and harmful idealization rather than observation and description. They translated cultural expectations into medical discourse in a highly manipulative way, placing science in the service of ideology in order to maintain male privilege rather than women's health.

Considering the tone, wit and insight of Woolf's letters alone, clearly, she would not have made a suitable patient for Mitchell's rest cure, incapable of accepting this over-bearing and reductive view of women. The medical construction of the female body as inferior, reproductive and ornamental in purpose was the body Woolf struggled to resist and revise, and the process and consequences of traditional courtship and romance were repellent to her. In 1906 at the age of twenty-four she complained of pressures to marry: "The world is full of kindness and stupidity, I wish everyone didn't tell me to marry. Is it crude human nature breaking out? I call it disgusting" (1:334). More bluntly, in 1907 she wrote to Lady Robert Cecil,

> [A]nyhow you dont have to contend with obscene old women, and young women too with beaks dripping gore, who advise you to marry. That is my daily penance, and has been these six months. "I think you should keep a maid Virginia—to do your hair—it makes such a difference—Men notice these things—not of course"—and so on and so on. Well, one of these days they shall have their paragraph—That is a terrible threat! (1:367)

Still, the pressures Woolf felt did not originate in these women, but are pressures woven tightly into sacred writings, classical texts, and institutional regulations. These "obscene old women, and young women too with beaks dripping gore" function as relay stations for coexistent and interlocking sets of statements dispersed throughout medical, legal, and religious discursive formations. The attempt by doctors to enforce these cultural attitudes was part of a larger movement to control female sexuality and domestic labor.

In *Three Guineas* Woolf described this diffuse movement and what's at stake:

> Chastity then as defined by St. Paul is seen to be a complex conception, based upon the love of long hair; the love of subjection; the love of an audience; the love of laying down the law, and, subconsciously, upon a very strong and natural desire that the woman's mind and body shall be reserved for the use of one man and one only. Such a conception when supported by the Angels,

nature, law, custom and the Church, and enforced by a sex with a strong personal interest to enforce it, and the economic means, was of undoubted power. The grip of its white if skeleton fingers can be found upon whatever page of history we open from St. Paul to Gertrude Bell. Chastity was invoked to prevent her from studying medicine; from painting from the nude; from reading Shakespeare; from playing in orchestras; from walking down Bond Street alone. [15]

How is it that Woolf understood so well the duplicity operating in these discourses? What is "good" for women—chastity, passivity, marriage, motherhood, domesticity—constitutes a powerful rhetoric, and essential to its success is its dependence on "Angels, nature, law, custom and the Church" to authorize and enforce the exploitation of women and their annihilation as socio-political agents. It is the argument of this chapter that Woolf's comprehensive understanding of patriarchal discourses and practices stemmed from her personal experiences with doctors, incest and mental breakdown in combination with her extensive reading and writing.

During Woolf's periods of illness, the doctors forbid or severely limited her reading and writing, and on four occasions between 1910 and 1915 she was sent to Burley, a private asylum in Twickenham, for the rest cure, a place Quentin Bell describes as a "kind of polite madhouse for female lunatics."[16] While under the care of Dr. Savage, Woolf wrote:

I long for a large room to myself, with books and nothing else, where I can shut myself up, and see no one, and read myself into peace. This would be possible at Gordon Sq: and nowhere else. I wonder why Savage doesn't see this. As a matter of fact my sleep hasn't improved a scrap since I have been here, and his sleeping draught gives me a headache, and nothing else.... [R]eally a doctor is worse than a husband! Oh how thankful I shall be to be my own mistress and throw their silly medicines down the slop pail! I never shall believe, or have believed, in anything any doctor says—I learnt their utter helplessness when Father was ill. (1:186)

In *Mrs. Dalloway* rather than an ethics of care, Woolf describes the doctor Sir William Bradshaw in terms of power, politics, and wealth:

Worshipping proportion, Sir William not only prospered himself but made

England prosper, secluded her lunatics, forbade childbirth, penalized despair, made it impossible for the unfit to propagate their views until they, too, shared his sense of proportion—his, if they were men, Lady Bradshaw's if they were women (she embroidered, knitted, spent four nights out of seven at home with her son).... Sir William with his thirty years' experience of these kinds of cases, and his infallible instinct, this is madness, this sense; his sense of proportion.[17]

Woolf's fictional Bradshaw might well represent Mitchell or Hyslop.

Ann Douglas Wood notes the common nineteenth-century attitude toward a sick woman: "If she could only have a child, it would cure her."[18] In 1926 in *The Principles and Practice of Endocrine Medicine,* William Berkeley wrote, "Woman, particularly, is largely under the sway of her sex hormones, and reaches perfect physical and mental development only after she has born a child."[19] The belief that women attained their holiest, most feminine and ideal state through pregnancy permeated a number of discourses, and, notwithstanding her radical perspective, it is unlikely that Woolf entirely escaped this pervasive view that pregnancy was necessary for fulfillment. In 1912 she wrote to Violet Dickinson, "next year I must have a child" (1:633). Dr. Savage, the Stephen family doctor who had known Virginia since her birth, told Leonard Woolf that pregnancy would do "her a world of good." However, Leonard, still uneasy with the idea, consulted other doctors, and in *Beginning Again,* he described how the decision to remain childless was made:

We both wanted to have children.... I went and consulted Sir George Savage; he brushed my doubts aside.... So I went off and consulted two other well known doctors, Maurice Craig and T. B. Hyslop, and also the lady who ran the mental nursing home where Virginia had several times stayed. They confirmed my fears and were strongly against her having children. We followed their advice.[20]

While there were powerful societal pressures on Woolf to achieve fulfillment through childbirth, it appears that Leonard was intent on gathering enough support to prevent such a possibility. Thus, Woolf lost control of her body regarding this important decision.

Earlier in her life, in another critical way, Woolf also lost control. From the age of six or seven to around the age of twenty-two, she was sexually abused by her half-brothers Gerald and George Duckworth. She described these events in presentations to the Memoir Club, in *Letters* and autobiographical writings, making clear her desire that the incest become a part of her official biography.[21] Roger Poole discusses the effects of the incest in *The Unknown Virginia Woolf*, published in 1978, and Louise DeSalvo makes the incest the focus of her biography, *Virginia Woolf: The Impact of Childhood Sexual Abuse on Her Life and Work*, published in 1989.[22]

Quentin Bell, Woolf's nephew, published his biography in 1972. His treatment of the incest differs from Poole's and DeSalvo's, and for over two decades the majority of reviewers have credited Bell's "insider's view" as the "truth."[23] Leonard Woolf had placed the Monk's House Papers at the disposal of Bell to use while writing Woolf's biography, and, of course, Bell had to acknowledge the evidence of incest present in the Monk's House Papers as well as the *Letters*. Still, in his discussion of this aspect of Woolf's life, he diminished its significance and shifted the responsibility. A brief examination of Bell's rhetoric as well as that of Nigel Nicolson (Vita Sackville-West's son and editor of Woolf's *Letters*) regarding the incest is important to this discussion. Like the religious, legal and medical discourses quoted earlier, this biographical discourse provides another example of the specific strategies used in the deployment of patriarchy. It is the attitudes and power structure embedded in these discourses that Woolf (along with Brontë and Eliot) identified and struggled to reveal and transform.

Under "Duckworth" in the index of Quentin Bell's biography, there is an entry entitled "George, incestuous relationship with VW." Also, Bell includes brief excerpts from Woolf's own descriptions of the events within two footnotes.[24] In spite of the evidence, Bell writes: "George Duckworth was the model brother. The eldest...he was twenty-seven, very handsome, comfortably well-off, pleasant, urbane and generous. His devotion to his half-sisters was exemplary.... After their mother's death his kindness knew no bounds...his arms were open for their relief."[25] In contrast to Bell's depiction of George as the "model brother," Woolf described George as "abnormally stupid," and "if you looked at him closely you noticed that one of his ears was pointed; and the other round; you also noticed that though he had the curls of a God and the ears of a faun he had unmistakably the eyes of a pig."[26] Clearly, Bell and Woolf disagree over the meaning of "George Duckworth."

In describing the incest in the main text, Bell writes, "Eros came with a commotion of leathern wings, a figure of mawkish incestuous sexuality. Virginia felt that George had spoilt her life before it had fairly begun."[27] Rather than saying that George came, Bell makes "eros" the subject of the sentence—the actor and the agent. In writing that "Virginia felt that George had spoilt her life"—by making Virginia the subject of this sentence—Bell shifts the responsibility from George onto Virginia. Rather than George's incestuous behavior, Bell makes Woolf's feelings the cause of her problem.

Again shifting the responsibility, Bell refers to Woolf as "naturally shy in sexual matters." He goes on to say, "I do not know enough about Virginia's mental illnesses to say whether this adolescent trauma was in any was connected with them," adding:

> In later years Virginia's and Vanessa's friends were a little astonished at the unkind mockery, the downright virulence, with which the sisters referred to their half-brother. He seemed to be a slightly ridiculous but on the whole an inoffensive old buffer, and so, in a sense, he was. His public face was amiable. But to his half-sisters he stood for something horrible and obscene, the final element of foulness in what was already an appalling situation.[28]

"To his half-sisters" George Duckworth stood for something horrible, but Bell carefully marks his different evaluation of George as devoted to his half-sisters with arms always "open for their relief." In doing so, Bell discredits Woolf's account, strongly implying that she was somehow mistaken and irrational in her response to the incest.

Interestingly enough, in the introduction to Woolf's *Letters,* Nigel Nicolson criticizes Bell for his "condemnation" of Duckworth. Nicolson writes:

> Let *us* imagine what may have occurred. At that time the two young men were sharing the house at Hyde Park Gate with two exceptionally pretty girls, *related to them only through their dead mother*. If George and Gerald did caress their half-sisters occasionally, perhaps lean over their desks or their beds to stroke their hair and shoulders, it would not seem to us unnatural nor too shocking. But to the girls, especially to Virginia, who was exceptionally

modest, it would appear appalling in retrospect.... [emphasis added] (xvi–xvii)

George and Gerald were related to their "exceptionally pretty" half-sisters "only through their dead mother." Any touching and stroking "would not seem to us unnatural nor too shocking." In beginning the sentence "Let us imagine," Nicolson wants to think for "us," and he not only denies the sexual abuse, but he also shifts the blame based on the obvious and irresistible temptation of such "exceptionally pretty girls."

Quentin Bell and Nigel Nicolson have had considerable control over the narrative of Woolf's life and letters. Their discursive accounts of her experiences with incest—so different from her own accounts—are noteworthy because, like the doctors, they provide examples of how the material of language can be used to maintain male privilege. By shifting responsibility onto the women and by using a tone of understanding and tolerance when discussing the half-brothers, Bell and Nicolson repeat and consolidate old and well established views regarding female bodies and sexual abuse. However unintentionally, in their repetitions Bell and Nicolson affirm and perpetuate both the attitudes and the abuse.

In Woolf's extended family, there were four daughters and four sons, and the evidence suggests that all four daughters were abused in some way. DeSalvo tells the story of Laura, who was twelve years older than Virginia and Leslie's daughter from his first marriage, and this story might explain why Stella, Vanessa, and Virginia could not make public their abuse while Leslie and Julia Stephen were alive. There was a change in Laura's behavior when the Duckworth and Stephen households were combined, and given "the fact of Virginia's and Vanessa's own sexual abuse, it is appropriate to wonder if Gerald or George Duckworth also molested Laura. Some of Laura's symptoms—choking, rages, doing poorly at reading even though she knew how to read—are known to be symptoms of sexual abuse."[29]

DeSalvo persuasively argues that Laura was not insane, but after the death of her mother and the subsequent cruelty of her father and stepmother, she was a child with problems. In his contemporary accounts Leslie described Laura's behavior as "sluggishness" and "mulishness," and he said she "lacked any moral sense" and was "vain." At the age of seven she spat meat out of her mouth, and as a teenager she suffered from nervous tics and speech impediments. What might be seen as her resistance and refusal to be dominated met—in Mitchell-like fashion—with isolation and bedrest. For Leslie, however, this isolation was not severe enough. Medication was used, and she was isolated in a different part of the house. Then, at the age of twenty-one Laura was sent to an asylum. It seems probable that this isolation and institutionalization may have sent a clear message to the other Stephen children.

Laura Stephen, although she knew how to read, refused to do so, and Leslie found this refusal "intensely provoking." DeSalvo writes that every time Virginia knocked on her father's study door and asked for another book "she was proving that she was not Laura; she was keeping herself from being called perverse; she was buying the right to live a life within the family."[30] Leslie Stephen came to believe that Virginia was "clearly destined for his own profession."[31] Based on Bell's and DeSalvo's accounts, it is possible to say that initially Woolf became an avid reader to escape the incestuous atmosphere of the Stephen household and escape Laura's fate. In a new fragment of "A Sketch of the Past," Woolf herself wrote of the connection between reading and her father:

> There was something we had in common. "What have you got hold of," he would say looking over my shoulder at the book I was reading; and how proud, priggishly, I was, if he gave his little amused, surprised snort, when he found me reading some book that no child my age could understand. I was a snob no doubt, and read partly to make him think me a very clever little brat.[32]

Based upon this reflection, it is possible that Woolf became an avid and precocious reader to please her father, obtain his protection, and create a safe space within this large and intimidating Victorian family.

Certainly, Woolf fell in love with words at an early age. Characterizing her reading as "addicted, escapist and ambitious," Lee writes that she "was reading avidly, from very early on, under the guidance of her father, and from eleven or twelve reading became her secret life, her 'habit,' and her refuge."[33] The numerous and diverse books she was reading at the age of fifteen are revealing.[34] Her father said, "Gracious, child, how you gobble," as he handed her "the sixth or seventh volume of Gibbon, or Spedding's *Bacon* or Cowper's Letters." Also, it was at this time that Woolf was given the freedom to select

her own books from her father's extensive library. Her letters
overflow with references to authors and books and to the study of
Latin and Greek. At the age of nineteen, rather than wanting to
dance, she wanted to read herself "blue in the nose" (1:36). About her
social life she wrote,

> Our London season about which you ask, was of the dullest description. I
> only went to three dances—and I think nothing else. But the truth of it is, as
> we frequently tell each other, we are failures. Really, we cant shine in Society.
> I dont know how its done. We aint popular—we sit in corners and look like
> mutes who are longing for a funeral. However, there are more important things
> in this life—from all I hear I shant be asked to dance in the next, and that is
> one of the reasons why I hope to go there. This is the kind of thing I say to
> Dorothea and she glows like a sunset over Mont Blanc. (1:37)

Instead of dancing around ballrooms, Woolf rummaged around the
London Library: "I got into the vaults where they keep the Times
yesterday, and had to be fished out by a man" (1:57). While she may
have begun to construct herself as a reader out of a need for
protection and safety, reading soon became a means to an awakening.

The actual tools Woolf used in handling the material of language—
her pens, ink, books, and writing desk—became precious to her, and
her affection shows itself in her descriptions:

> I wish you could see my room at this moment, on a dark winter's evening—all
> my beloved leather backed books standing up so handsome in their shelves,
> and a nice fire, and the electric light burning, and a huge mass of manuscripts
> and letters and proof-sheets and pens and inks over the floor and everywhere.
> Tomorrow week they will be bad enough for a general clearance; then I start
> tidy and gradually work myself up into a happy frenzy of litter. (1:202)

In 1903 at twenty-one, Woolf thanks her brother Thoby for a
birthday gift:

> You are an angel to have routed out a Montaigne for me. I was getting quite
> desperate. I have hunted him 3 years. This one is better than a Florio I think—
> I once had a chance of a 2nd Edition Florio in my penniless days—I may have
> told you the story—but it is a badly printed book, very black and close, and I
> dont think there is much to choose between the translations. I always read

Montaigne in bed, and these books will do beautifully. The Bacon is one of
my choicest works—especially the note on the title page. I havent got a copy,
so I shall stick to these; it looks to me as though it had worn its corners
round in some coat pocket. I shall carry it in my fur coat many a mile and many
a mile—Yours are the only books I had given me. Gerald gave me a
magnificent pearl necklace—which I smashed first thing, all my other presents
were jewels of some kind. (1:66)

The excerpt reveals her knowledge of the production, appearance and
value of books and her attention to how words appear on the page.
The way she described carrying the book in her pocket might well be
the way one describes walking with a dear friend. She desired books
and was excited by the thought of possessing them:

There is a book I have long had my eye on which I shall now buy the first
moment I am in London, and I am already rather excited about it. (1:204)

I should be rather sorry to end my solitude. It is amazingly comfortable to
stretch ones legs and have one's read out, and not to be interrupted at half
past six, and spend the evening at the opera, or in talk about it. I never knew I
had such a desire to read; and in London it is always fretted and stinted, and
always will be. I wish one could sweep ones days clean; say not at home, and
refuse ever to go out. (1:444)

In a letter to Roger Fry she described the experience of reading
Proust:

My great adventure is really Proust. Well—what remains to be written after
that? I'm only in the first volume, and there are, I suppose, faults to be found,
but I am in a state of amazement; as if a miracle were being done before my eyes.
How, at last, has someone solidified what has always escaped—and made it
too into this beautiful and perfectly enduring substance? One has to put the
book down and gasp. The pleasure becomes physical—like sun and wine and
grapes and perfect serenity and intense vitality combined. (2:565–66)

Woolf's pleasure in pens and books indicates the significance of
language use in her life—"this beautiful and perfectly enduring
substance"—and also reveals the devastating consequences of the rest
cure's ban on reading and writing.

In describing reading as an adventure and a pleasure that becomes "physical—like sun and wine and grapes," Woolf described it as a visceral encounter and transaction that takes place between words and body. Surely, Woolf valued and was deeply engaged in and affected by her reading experiences. George Eliot wrote that those who "read to any purpose" cannot help being modified by the ideas that pass through the mind.[35] Still, one might ask if all readers, like Woolf, are "modified" by their reading? What distinction is Eliot making between those who read and those who do not read "to any purpose"?

Woolf seems to answer these important questions concerning the process of reading through the character of Clarissa Dalloway in *The Voyage Out*. According to Clarissa herself, she is a great reader, especially of literature, but how is she affected by this reading? Although she only appears in three early chapters of *The Voyage Out*, "Clarissa, indeed, is a fascinating spectacle."[36] With care, Woolf arranges concentric circles of material things around Clarissa; her body is "wrapped in furs, her head in veils." She carries a "dressing-case suggestive of diamond necklaces and bottles with silver tops," and surrounding her are many "solid leather bags of a rich brown hue" (40). Covered with white cloth, followed by the scent of violets, surrounded by the sounds of rustling skirts and tinkling necklaces, she appears "astonishingly" like an "eighteenth-century masterpiece—a Reynolds or a Romney" (47). The narrator comments that not an inch of her person lacks its proper instrument, and maintaining her ornamental body takes great quantities of money, time, and energy.

In the short space of two chapters Clarissa refers to *Antigone*, Shakespeare, Shelley, Jane Austen, *Wuthering Heights*, and the Brontës; she quotes from *Adonais* and goes to bed with Pascal, "which went with her everywhere" (52). However, upon closer examination, one sees that Clarissa garbles the Shelley quote and uses Pascal as a sleeping pill, the same way her husband uses Jane Austen. The scene of reading is neither an experiment or a dialogue for Clarissa, not a place to put values into play or a field of study creating questions and provoking controversy. Rather, she uses literature in the way she uses other material objects, like her clothes, scents, jewelry, and furs, to fill and maintain the space between her body and others. She fills this space with the sounds of impressive literary titles, and her remarks are said "with her usual air of saying something profound" (55).

What things does this "spectacle" of womanhood know and say? She knows that "scholars married any one—girls they met in farms on reading parties; or little suburban women who said disagreeably, 'Of course I know it's my husband you want; not *me*.'" She knows that musicians with long hair are bad musicians, and that in general men always *are* so much better than women. She knows that she "*must* have a son*,*" and she knows that "one couldn't bear *not* to be English!" She is positive that her husband is right in condemning the suffragists, in his words "the utter folly and futility of such behaviour...well! may I be in my grave before a woman has the right to vote in England!" When Helen disagrees with Clarissa, there is an uncomfortable pause, and Clarissa shivers and asks for her fur cloak. As she adjusts "the soft brown fur about her neck," she regains her composure and begins anew: "I own...that I shall never forget the *Antigone*." Her comments rarely move beyond emotional ejaculation and a bit of description: "there's almost everything one wants in 'Adonais'" and isn't *Antigone* "the most modern thing you ever saw?" The one time she engages in analysis, she compares her feeling for her husband with what women of her mother's generation felt for Christ (41-52).

Clarissa's attractiveness, social status, and wealth along with her total endorsement of male supremacy make her one of the chosen few who represent, from a patriarchal perspective, what all women should be. She makes "Helen and the others look coarse and slovenly beside her," and her scent attracts all the men on the ship (47). The space surrounding Clarissa, complete with sounds, smells, colors, and fancy literary titles, marks and certifies her as a "true woman." This filled space is both a sign of her status and the material practice of performing certain sounds and words that announce and consolidate this status. As a material practice, the filled space creates a barrier where there was none, constricting and constraining while at the same time seeming to protect, enhance and beautify. An expensive advertisement and an enforcer of the patriarchal code, Clarissa constitutes the injunction to femininity and, at the same time, as Woolf's fictional creation, a parody of it.

As a participant in the patriarchal code, Clarissa refuses to see the contradictions in her style of living. She is both the exemplary bourgeois subject and, as she tells the reader dramatically, concerned with poverty. She never gets beyond appearances, ignoring the contradiction between the oppressive relations of production necessary to keep her in furs and smelling like violets and her concern for poverty, living in what Woolf describes as "a kind of nondescript cotton wool.... A great part of every day is not lived consciously. One walks, eats, sees things, deals with what has to be done."[37] Through Clarissa, Woolf repeats a type—the upper-middle class married woman as ornament—to analyze it and politicize its effects.

What Clarissa fails to recognize through her reading, Woolf does recognize. At twenty-one, Woolf writes to her intimate friend Violet Dickinson, "Have you any stays? I tried to saw mine through this morning, but couldnt. What iron boned conventionality we live in—stays suggest many lively thoughts" (1:89). Moving far beyond the ideology of her parents, Woolf deals in shocks and blows that are "a token of some real thing behind appearances; and I make it real by putting it into words. It is only by putting it into words that I make it whole."[38] Her psyche mediates experience and language, her psyche as active and dynamic, working to combine, shift, alter, and create her own philosophy.

V. N. Volosinov locates the psyche—not a transcendental core but the effect of social experience—on the borderline between the organism and the outside world. The psyche is composed of the material of signs, and the inner sign is "preeminently" inner speech.[39] A human being acquires consciousness *only* in social interaction: "the content of the individual psyche is by its very nature just as social as is ideology, and the very degree of consciousness of one's individuality and its inner rights and privileges is ideological, historical, and wholly conditioned by sociological factors."[40]

In the first pages of *The Voyage Out*, as if to convey in novelistic discourse the idea that one's "individuality" is ideological, historical, and wholly conditioned by sociological factors, Woolf blurs the traditional distinctions and boundaries among bodies, bodies and things, and inner and outer worlds. As Helen and her husband Ridley make their way toward the ship, angry glances strike their backs. It is a dismal and gloomy atmosphere in tune with Helen's melancholy, and Helen's mind is "like a wound exposed to dry in the air." The narrator comments, "When one gave up seeing the beauty that clothed things, this was the skeleton beneath." On the ship the sight of town and river are still present in Helen's mind. Rachel nervously awaits their arrival, looking forward to seeing them "as though they were of the nature of an approaching physical discomfort,—a tight shoe or a draughty window." The second sentence out of Ridley's mouth is "Ah! she's not like her mother," and the irritating words cause Rachel's face to blush "scarlet" (11–15). These early instances of interaction between signifying acts and body—glances that strike, minds like exposed wounds, words that turn the skin scarlet—destroy any notion of impenetrability. In this immeasurable fluidity and commerce between bodies and glances and language, bodily outline is not circumscription, but a place of contact and interchange.

Like the psyche, experience exists *only* in the material of signs; we "do not see or feel an experience—we understand it. This means that in the process of introspection we engage our experience into a context made up of other signs we understand. A sign can be illuminated only with the help of another sign."[41] Volosinov's discourse is helpful in understanding Woolf's personal movement from victim to agent and from an upper-middle class daughter to a radical writer. Reading and writing widely—made possible in Woolf's case by her father's library—and with a purpose furnish the psyche with a number of discourses, each with its own diction, beliefs, and rules. The psyche may shift and grow as more discourses are assimilated and contrasted with what is already known.

Discursive agency takes place in these instances of speech interchange: it is "in the inner working of this verbally materialized social psychology, that *the barely noticeable shifts and changes that will later find expression in fully fledged ideological products accumulate*" [emphasis added].[42] The "shifts and changes" occur in internal conversations and debates where the distrust, struggle, recombinations and hybridization of ideas, beliefs, and values result in an altered point of view. These "barely noticeable shifts and changes" found the discursive agency at work in Woolf's subversive repetitions. The value of reading emerges in this dynamic process of interaction between psyche and outer world, and through continued reading one acquires a variety of semiotic materials, making possible internal dialogue and innovative knowledge production.

In her introduction to *Moments of Being,* Jeanne Schulkind discusses a distinction Woolf made between types of people:

In both the memoirs and in the novels there are figures around whom precise outlines are drawn, in contrast to the supple, fluid lines which she commonly used to portray character. Such figures are so encrusted with the trivia of daily life, so attached to objects and values which are in the last analysis irrelevant, or so imprisoned by their egocentricity, that they are incapable of cutting themselves from the material world.... Reality never penetrates the cotton wool of their daily lives.[43]

Clarissa can only consolidate the finely-tuned system of male privilege and its subsequent unequal and oppressive relations of power among economic classes and between men and women. Her "happiness" necessitates exploitation and the bigotry necessary to justify the exploitation.

Woolf could have been a Clarissa Dalloway. She had the parents, the physical beauty, and the social status to do so. Lee writes that around the age of 42 Woolf came "to be photographed and caricatured and glamorised. By the end of 1924 she was in a position (as she remembered Leslie wanting to be) 'to know everyone worth knowing.'"[44] Woolf liked being fashionably dressed and was thought to be somewhat of a snob, but, more importantly for her readers, she became a socialist, a pacifist, and a feminist, and in her writing she performed experiments in language that interrupt and displace traditional patterns and scripts. Through self-reflexivity and analysis, Woolf's satire displays in detail the thoughts, speech, dress, and gestures of the middle and upper classes. Her radical point of view and cultural critique emanate from a central position within the very culture she criticized. Through her experiences as a reader and writer, Woolf was able to transmute baser personal experiences and the books in her father's library into narratives that refused reductive views of women, introducing instead numerous and diverse women with distinct bodies, beliefs and desires.

Rachel's Voyage Out

Women's only purpose is to bear children.

Thomas Aquinas
Summa Theologiae

Look at the numerous families of girls in this neighbourhood.... The brothers of these girls are every one in business or in professions; they have something to do: their sisters have no earthly employment, but household work and sewing; no earthly pleasure, but an unprofitable visiting; and no hope, in all their life to come, of anything better. This stagnant state of things makes them decline in health: they are never well; and their minds and views shrink to wondrous narrowness.

Charlotte Brontë
Shirley

Despite the complexity of causes behind Woolf's prolific reading discussed in the previous chapter, it is clear that in her writing she increasingly confronted and analyzed the personal relationships she would escape or strengthen. More and more she would create other spaces to inhabit, spaces not saturated with romantic love, betrayal, violation, or the need for approval. In 1906 Woolf explained this desire in a letter to Madge Vaughan:

My only defence is that I write of things as I see them; and I am quite conscious all the time that it is a very narrow, and rather bloodless point of view. I think...I could explain a little why this is so from *external* reasons; such as education, way of life etc. And so perhaps I may get something better as I grow older. George Eliot was near 40 I think, when she wrote her first novel....

But my present feeling is that this vague and dream like world, without love, or heart, or passion, or sex, is the world I really care about, and find interesting. For, though they are dreams to you, and I cant express them at all adequately, these things are perfectly real to me. [original emphasis] (1:272)

In a letter written in the same month to Violet Dickinson, Woolf continued:

Madge tells me I have no heart—at least in my writing: really I begin to get alarmed. If marriage is necessary to one's style, I shall have to think about it. There is some truth in it, isn't there?—but not the whole truth. And there is something indecent, to my virgin mind, in a maiden having that kind of heart. "The air is full of it" says Madge: but I breathe something else. (1:273)

Woolf often referred to this "something else," to her wish to "capture multitudes of things at present fugitive, enclose the whole, and shape infinite strange shapes" (1:438). She spent seven years writing her first novel *The Voyage Out*, and the world she described in these excerpts—that dream-like world, without love, heart, passion or sex, that something else she breathes—takes shape around and in the unusual character of Rachel Vinrace. Her physical journey from England to the island of Santa Marina in Brazil frames a double story, and this chapter examines Rachel's voyage out through personal growth and development and her parallel voyage into the closed space of courtship and marriage.

Woolf may have started thinking of *The Voyage Out* as early as 1904 after the death of her father. In 1908 she began to talk frequently about it in her letters and worked with the novel through no fewer than seven and perhaps as many as eleven or twelve drafts. When the novel begins, Rachel, who is twenty-four and a classical pianist, has been living in Richmond with two maiden aunts. Along with another aunt, Helen Ambrose, Rachel travels by ship to Brazil and first meets Terence Hewet and St. John Hirst at the hotel in Santa Marina.

At first, there is a strange and exciting intimation that these four people are in love, that unusual amounts of sexual tension, intellectual stimulation, and affection exist *among them*. The coupling keeps slipping as Helen is attracted to Rachel, St. John to Terence, St. John to Helen, and Terence to Rachel. After the ball, Terence's thoughts move from Rachel to thoughts of Rachel and Helen as he wonders "whether he was in love with them or not."[1] Other characters repeat and reinforce this slippage. Evelyn says, "What I want you to tell me is, can one be in love with two people at once, or can't one?" (190). Ridley states, "Hirst and Hewet, they're all the same to me" (196). Mrs. Flushing feels it "might have been either of them…both frightened her" (234). And Rachel responds to Terence and St. John as one entity capable of altering her sense of reality: "Hewet and Hirst appeared…. Rachel's heart beat hard. She was conscious of an extraordinary intensity in everything, as though their presence stripped some cover off the surface of things" (200). As the friendships progress, however, there seems to be an external force that mandates that things must become traditional, that Rachel must mate with one of the men.

Helen "had been thinking about Rachel and which of the two young men she was likely to fall in love with" (205). St. John tells Terence, "I rather think Rachel's in love with me…. That's the worst of friendships with young women—they tend to fall in love with one" (238). After Rachel first thinks she might be in love with Terence, she feels "much as a soldier prepared for battle" (176). Still, she never stops to consider what will happen if she continues in this way, "so that Helen's image of the river sliding on to the waterfall had a great likeness to the facts" (223).

The text nicely marks a distinction between Rachel's attraction to Terence and such feelings in literature: "none of the books she read, from *Wuthering Heights* to *Man and Superman,* and the plays of Ibsen, suggested from their analysis of love that what their heroines felt was what she was feeling now. It seemed to her that her sensations had no name" (223). Yet, Rachel does not need to find words to express her feelings; the conventions of traditional romance supply the names and the appropriate phrases. Terence looks at Rachel "sometimes as if she must know that they were waiting together, and being drawn on together, without being able to offer any resistance" (267). Something else begins to manipulate this situation, prescribing appropriate words, feelings, and behavior.

Although Rachel likes being with Terence and at times gains more self-confidence through their conversations, she becomes increasingly disenchanted with what the institution of marriage will allow her to be. In a book about voyaging out, the trip becomes paradoxically a voyaging into marital confinement. Her voyage becomes a voyage away from her private space, but that private space is just what she values most. Her most peaceful productive moments are moments spent in the solitude of her room.

There is a reference to Rachel's piano in her attic room in Richmond, and when first introduced in the novel, she is in one of the ship's rooms with a piano and several books scattered over the floor. She spends hours alone, thinking, daydreaming, reading German and a little English, or playing the difficult music of Bach, Beethoven, Mozart and Purcell. Woolf returns to Rachel's love of private space a third time and in some detail at Santa Marina. Helen had promised Rachel a room "cut off from the rest of the house, large, private—a room in which she could play, read, think, defy the world, a fortress as well as a sanctuary" (123).

Like the majority of well-to-do girls in the second half of the nineteenth century, Rachel's education was less than satisfactory: "The shape of the earth, the history of the world, how trains worked, or money was invested, what laws were in force...none of this had been imparted to her" (34). The one advantage of this lack of education is that all her energies flowed into her music, and the narrator makes it clear that she is a gifted pianist. Rachel is fanatical about her music, and Marianne DeKoven notes that "Woolf has developed her piano playing throughout the novel as the locus of her modernist heroism, her capacity for profound, difficult, unconventional, authentic behavior and expression."[2] Rachel might have been a concert pianist, and perhaps the first thing one should do to understand her is to listen to classical music, to a Bach fugue in A or a Beethoven sonata. But her relatives give her little if any encouragement. Her Aunt Bessie fears practicing too much will spoil her arms, and her father tells Helen, "She's...devoted to her music—a little less of *that* would do no harm" [original emphasis] (85).

Except for the classical music, Rachel's past life appears dry and gloomy. Early in the narrative when asked if she ever reads, she responds, *"Cowper's Letters*—that kind of thing. Father gets them for me or my Aunts" (80). Her only girlfriend, a religious zealot reminiscent of Helen Burn, likes to talk of how best to take up one's cross. Her father likes the idea of her staying with Helen since he plans to become a member of Parliament and wants Rachel to help with dinners and evening parties. Helen laughs "at the notion of it—Rachel as Tory hostess!" and marvels at the "astonishing ignorance" of her father (86). At the age of twenty-four Rachel knows nothing about sexual relations; she doesn't even know how children are produced. Helen writes in a letter, "It seems to me not merely foolish but criminal to bring people up like that," and Helen will assume the role of Rachel's maternal guide (96).

Because Helen is both a survivor and an enabler of patriarchal culture, what kind of a guide can she make? Since she has servants, she is free from the tasks of cleaning, cooking, grocery shopping, and raising children, and because of the kind of husband she has, she can maintain a distinct sense of freedom and separateness in her marriage. Although she appears deeply saddened at the thought of leaving her children for a year, she later says, "I'd much rather be a cook than a nurse.... Nothing would induce me to take charge of children" (43). Still, Helen strongly feels that "wife and mother" are the correct roles for women. Excused because of her class and beauty from the tedious and often harsh realities of domestic chores, Helen's day-to-day existence consolidates the patriarchal structure, and thus, she functions as an enabler.

During dinner Helen and Rachel—"after the fashion of their sex, highly trained in promoting men's talk without listening to it"—do not speak. Upon leaving the dining room and glancing back, *both* see Mr. Pepper "as though he had suddenly loosened his clothes, and had become a vivacious and malicious old ape" (17). Moments later Rachel compares Mr. Pepper to a fossilized fish, saying his "heart's a piece of old shoe leather," but Helen responds, "I expect you're too severe" (19). One of the Richmond aunts has written Helen about Rachel spoiling her arms by practicing the piano, and Rachel asks, "The muscles of the forearm—and then one won't marry?" Although this is the aunt's fear, Helen answers, "She didn't put it quite like that." Twice Helen as wife-mother-aunt checks Rachel's tendency to question authority, demanding instead compromise and acquiescence; and twice during this conversation Woolf inserts "Mrs. Ambrose" rather than "Helen" to emphasize Helen's complicity with the status quo.

Helen explains to Rachel that men will want to kiss her, will want to marry her, "you must take things as they are; and if you want friendship with men you must run risks" (81). But Rachel finds it "terrifying" and "disgusting," and her mind works "very quickly, inconsistently and painfully. Helen's words hewed down great blocks which had stood there always, and the light which came in was cold." Rachel bursts out, "So that's why I can't walk alone!... Because men are brutes! I hate men!" Educational and professional constraints pale in contrast to the threatening nature of male sexuality, and the narrator comments:

> By this new light she saw her life for the first time a creeping hedged-in thing, driven cautiously between high walls, here turned aside, there plunged in darkness, made dull and crippled for ever—her life that was the only chance she had—the short season between two silences. (82)

Helen counsels "how to be a reasonable person," how to keep things in proportion. Later at Santa Marina, Helen writes: "I have taken it upon myself to enlighten her, and now, though still a good deal prejudiced and liable to exaggerate, she is more or less a reasonable human being" (96). Relying on words like "enlighten" and "reasonable," Helen wants to mold Rachel into someone like herself. Such manipulation tempered with genuine affection echoes back to accounts of Julia Stephen's relationship with her daughters and will repeat itself in Mrs. Ramsay's relationship with Lily Briscoe and Minta Doyle in *To the Lighthouse*. Interestingly enough, Woolf provides no clues as to how Rachel feels about Helen, but Rachel's love of solitude remains. Her most peaceful, productive moments are those moments spent alone.

For Rachel, the Santa Marina room becomes an "enchanted place, where the poets sang and things fell into their right proportions" (123). She does not think of men or dream of love and marriage in this private space, but appears—much like Woolf in her descriptions of her own privacy—satisfied and happy. Rachel states that she will never marry (60), and might well have written what Woolf wrote in a letter: "The only thing in this world is music—music and books and one or two pictures. I am going to found a colony where there shall be no marrying—unless you happen to fall in love with a symphony of Beethoven" (1:35). Also in this third private space on Santa Marina, Rachel changes her reading habits. Whereas before she did not much care for books, here, free of the censorship of her father and aunts, she becomes an avid reader—"for the moment music was deserted" (123).

Reading the *Works of Henrik Ibsen,* "her eyes were concentrated almost sternly upon the page...her whole body was constrained by the working of her mind. At last she shut the book sharply, lay back, and drew a deep breath, expressive of the wonder which always marks the transition from the imaginary world to the real world" (123). These intense reading experiences stay with her and enter her psyche, her very being. She acts the parts of Ibsen's plays for days, and then becomes Diana Merion in Meredith's *Diana of the Crossways.* Helen notes that it is not all acting, that "some sort of change was taking place in the human being." Helen "would have suggested Defoe, Maupassant, or some spacious chronicle of family life," but Rachel chooses modern books that to Helen are tokens "of harsh wrangling and disputes about facts which had no such importance as the moderns claimed for them. But she did not interfere" (124).

In contrast to spacious chronicles of family life, the Ibsen plays are harsh critiques of a woman's place in the family. In *A Doll's House* Nora Helmer leaves her husband and two children. In despair over her marriage and pregnancy, Hedda Gabler, in the play of the same name, commits suicide. These choices, rather than extolling the benefits of the compromise that Helen advocates, highlight the magnitude of the problem. Some sort of "change was taking place" as Rachel's "whole body was constrained by the working of her mind" during these reading experiences (123–24). This time alone reading is an active time when she engages the material of her psyche with the material on the printed page.

On the other hand, during discussions of love with Terence, Rachel often repeats what he says as though she is trying to learn the script: "'We love each other,' Terence said. 'We love each other,' she repeated.... 'Terrible—terrible,' she murmured" (271). There is frequent uncertainty and questioning. Rachel says, "Am I in love—is this being in love—are we to marry each other?" (281). She answers the question, "Yes, I'm in love. There's no doubt.... It will be a fight" (282). Terence, with his own abundance of reluctance and ambivalence, says, "What's happened?... Why did I ask you to marry me? How did it happen?" Rachel responds, "Did you ask me to marry you?" (282). The continual repetition and questioning destroy any sense that this man and woman consciously and deliberately enter into the contract. For Rachel, the gap between liking someone—"those beautiful but too vast desires"—and fitting that liking into the institutional slots of engagement, marriage, and parenting is enormous (290).

Terence's reasons for wanting Rachel are directly opposed to her development as a thinker, a reader, and a musician. On the cliff Terence is "overcome with the desire to hold her in his arms," but Rachel begins to talk about music and "became less desirable as her brain began to work" (211–12). Rachel's piano playing symbolizes both the large independent space she has created, and her need for such a space, but when she tries to play a Beethoven sonata, Terence interrupts. She says, "No, Terence, it's no good; here am I, the best musician in South America, not to speak of Europe and Asia, and I can't play a note because of you...." He answers:

> You don't seem to realise that that's what I've been aiming at for the last half-hour.... I've no objection to nice, simple tunes—indeed, I find them very helpful to literary composition, but that kind of thing is merely like an unfortunate old dog going round on its hind legs in the rain. (292)

Terence, like her father, would have Rachel service his interests, would have her provide a stimulating environment for his work, his literary composition, in spite of the fact that Rachel is clearly a gifted pianist and Terence's gift has not yet revealed itself. Even worse, "that kind of thing"—Rachel playing a Beethoven sonata—is likened to "an unfortunate old dog on its hind legs in the rain." Not quite a new metaphor, Terence reiterates Samuel Johnson's notorious remark that a woman's preaching is like a dog's walking on his hind legs.[3] Repeating the metaphor in a new context, the text establishes a sense of the continuity of sexist attitudes as well as revealing more of Terence's character. We see what kind of a husband he is becoming even before the marriage ceremony: he will certainly assume the dominant role, will take full advantage of male privilege, and will smother Rachel in the process.

When Rachel identifies her feeling as liking, Terence corrects her: "You fell in love with me," and she responds, "No, I never fell in love, if falling in love is what people say it is, and it's the world that tells the lies and I tell the truth. Oh, what lies—what lies!" (293). Here Rachel revises the narrative, clearly stating her refusal of traditional romantic love. In a subsequent conversation, Terence says, "you'll never see it!...because with all your virtues you don't, and you never will, care with every fibre of your being for the pursuit of truth! You've no respect for facts, Rachel; you're essentially feminine" (295). Rather than listening and comprehending what Rachel is trying to communicate, Terence, more and more, speaks patriarchal platitudes. The text explicitly marks Rachel and Terence as very different, and the difference becomes more obvious as their affection becomes formalized and transformed into an engagement (283).

In *The Voyage Out* the diction and metaphors that run throughout the courtship and engagement convey a sense of confrontation, inevitability, force, and aversion. This marriage will be a "fight" between Rachel's exploration and expression of her space in the world and the forces working through Terence and Helen to thrust her into the role of wife and mother. Terence tells her, "We must have a son and we must have a daughter." Referring to the pile of congratulatory letters, he tells her, "you ought to be answering these." The letters of congratulation add to the formulaic sense of what is happening to her: "It was strange, considering how very different these people were, that they used almost the same sentences when they wrote to congratulate her upon her engagement" (293–95). And, significantly, when she does begin to write the thank-you notes, she finds her phrases very much like the letters she has condemned.

As an example of a repetition with no difference, this writing situation articulates no agency. Rachel, unable to write or speak herself out of the ritual, looks around the room at the bed, the window-pane, the branches of a tree, and is amazed "at the gulf which lay between all that and her sheet of paper" (296). Terence tells her she must go to tea with Mrs. Thornbury, and she responds, "I'd rather have my right hand sawn in pieces—just imagine! the eyes of all those women!" (308). Terence expects a strict conformity, and *in life* Rachel cannot escape conforming to his expectations. She goes to tea with Mrs. Thornbury.

Woolf, in her own experiences, knew well the impossibility of escaping social scripts. In 1911 she wrote to Vanessa, "I could not write, and all the devils came out—the hairy black ones. To be 29 and unmarried—to be a failure—childless—insane too, no writer" (1:570). In the same year, Leonard Woolf began to pursue her, but she was openly ambivalent about him and about marriage. Terence tells

Rachel, "I don't satisfy you in the way you satisfy me.... There's something I can't get hold of in you. You don't want me as I want you—you're always wanting something else" (302). Woolf wrote to Leonard, "I sometimes think that if I married you, I could have everything—and then—is it the sexual side of it that comes between us? As I told you brutally the other day, I feel no physical attraction in you. There are moments—when you kissed me the other day was one—when I feel no more than a rock" (1:615). In spite of the tremendous pressures to marry, Woolf had refused four marriage proposals prior to Leonard's. She finally accepted his, and they were married in 1912.

About Rachel's illness and death, DeSalvo notes, "how painstakingly Woolf altered her text as the years went by and how she gradually introduced greater and greater symbolic significance by incorporating literary allusions containing analogues to Rachel's fate."[4] There are references to *Agamemnon,* later changed to *Antigone,* Sappho's *Ode to Aphrodite* that St. John reads during Mr. Bax's sermon, Milton's *Comus,* and Charles Kingsley's "A New Forest Ballad," among others. These allusions call to mind a number of women—Cassandra, Clytemnestra, Antigone, Sappho, the Lady, Sabrina, and Jane—and it is illuminating to think of why and how they died in relation to Rachel's death. In the case of Antigone, Sabrina, Jane, and perhaps Sappho, it is a self-willed death.

Rachel first becomes ill while Terence reads *Comus* aloud. In Milton's masque, Comus has placed a spell on the Lady, and when her brothers arrive, they fail to take Comus's wand, and so they must ask Sabrina for help. DeSalvo states that Sabrina only helps women who are pure, and so, "Rachel dies; she is not saved." DeSalvo believes that unlike the Lady in *Comus,* Rachel has not passed through her journey unscathed because early in the novel she "succumbed to the charms of Richard Dalloway."[5] On the contrary, Rachel's death can be read as death by choice rather than death as punishment. In another passage, DeSalvo herself writes that Rachel's death can be interpreted as an escape from marriage through death.[6]

Although Richard Dalloway is the first character to talk with Rachel and show an interest in her, this interest ends in his forcefully kissing her. The ship lurches, and Rachel falls forward: "Richard took her in his arms and kissed her. Holding her tight, he kissed her passionately, so that she felt the hardness of his body and the

roughness of his cheek printed upon hers. She fell back in her chair..."
(76). Rachel falls forward and backward, and it is important to
remember that at this point in the novel she does not even understand
sexuality. Richard attacks her with his passionate kissing, and then
says, "You tempt me." Like Bell, Richard shifts the responsibility to
the woman. After this collision, Rachel

> dreamt that she was walking down a long tunnel, which grew so narrow by
> degrees that she could touch the damp bricks on either side. At length the
> tunnel opened and became a vault; she found herself trapped in it, bricks
> meeting her wherever she turned, alone with a little deformed man who
> squatted on the floor gibbering, with long nails. The wall behind him oozed
> with damp, which collected into drops and slid down. (77)

Instead of saying Rachel did not pass through her journey unscathed
because she "succumbed to the charms of Richard Dalloway," it is
possible to interpret the analogy between Rachel and the Lady
differently. Like the Lady, Rachel remains separate from the
contamination around her; still, the contamination transposes its way
into her dreams. And, whereas at the end of *Comus* the Lady returns
to a safe space, Rachel has no such space. Her seducer Richard, her
father Willoughby, her fiancé Terence, her aunt Helen, and many of
the other married female characters stand as one in their attitude
toward marriage, linked by a shared understanding of "woman" and
blind to what Rachel can be.

Sabrina had to jump into the water to escape her tormentors, and
she "underwent a quick immortal change, / Made Goddess of the
River."[7] During her illness, Rachel "saw nothing and heard nothing but
a faint booming sound, which was the sound of the sea rolling over her
head. While all her tormentors thought that she was dead, she was not
dead, but curled up at the bottom of the sea" (341). Water is the
dominant image surrounding Rachel's death, signifying "fluidity,
softness, comfort, and absence of hardness or resistance." Water is
the antidote for the hardness of male abstraction, for the relentlessly
analytical attitude, the opposite of the hard kitchen table in *To The
Lighthouse* or the "beak of brass" that Roger Poole sees as the
archetype of male aggression in Woolf's writing.[8] When Rachel
regains consciousness a few days before her death:

> All sights were something of an effort, but the sight of Terence was the greatest effort, because he forced her to join mind to body in the desire to remember something. She did not wish to remember; it troubled her when people tried to disturb her loneliness; she wished to be alone. She wished for nothing else in the world. (347)

Rachel's "voyage out" has climaxed in this wish to be alone. In contrast, by entering into a marriage contract, her life would become a rigidly enforced ritual of sexual-social contact and performance. As Evelyn states within the novel, marriage would be a renunciation of

> all other men, and movement, and the real things of life. Love was all very well, and those snug domestic houses, with the kitchen below and the nursery above, which were so secluded and self-contained, like little islands in the torrents of the world; but the real things were surely the things that happened, the causes, the wars, the ideals, which happened in the great world outside, and went on independently of these women, turning so quietly and beautifully towards the men.... [T]here must be better things than that. Surely one could get nearer to life, one could get more out of life, one could enjoy more and feel more than they would ever do. (320)

In *The Voyage Out* Rachel's death by choice becomes her rite of refusal, what DeKoven calls her "only road to freedom."[9]

While older critics attribute Rachel's death to tropical fever or unwashed vegetables, a number of recent critics abandon this literal interpretation. After examining the Holograph and subsequent Typescripts of the novel and because "*everything is there not by chance, but by choice,*" Mitchell Leaska concludes that Rachel's "death...*is a self-willed death*" [original emphasis].[10] Madeline Moore writes: "Rachel's inability to retain her autonomy...signals her decision to capitulate to oblivion.... Her capitulation to illness, then, is the delirious expression of her chosen suicide."[11] In her discussion of *The Voyage Out* and *Heart of Darkness,* Rosemary Pitt refers to the "obvious death wish in Rachel, which seems to be caused chiefly by her sense of the transient nature of life, and the inadequacy of any human relationship."[12] Pitt blames Rachel rather than the larger socio-political situation, claiming that *Heart of Darkness* has an ethical dimension that *The Voyage Out* lacks: "one feels that Rachel's fears about life and her sense of horror at the idea of sex and marriage could be tamed and diluted through a successful union with Hewet and a consequent reduction in the scale of her desires, which have arisen partly through her immature confusion about what life involves."[13] But, Rachel is not confused, clearly understanding, as she does, what her married life would involve. In Pitt's wish that Rachel change, we see the medical attitude that illness and cure reside within the female body resurface and transpose itself into critical discourse. We see a demand that the woman compromise herself by reducing her desire. Also, rather than the novel lacking an ethical dimension, perhaps Pitt fails to grasp the novel's feminist ethics.

Like Ibsen's *A Doll's House* and *Hedda Gabler, The Voyage Out* does not ask a woman to change. By ending with female characters who choose to exit the scene, these artistic works ask rather that the female body stop being read as the cause of the problem, that the social scene be altered, that society reconsider its expectations based on sexual difference. Why should Rachel reduce her desire and play "nice simple tunes" to advance Terence's work? Why ask Rachel to accept this inferior position?

While several critics view Rachel's death as death by choice, Woolf's point is not to find fault with Rachel—in her venturing too far, her ambiguity about her sexual choice, or her "immature" confusion. The point is to find fault with a culture that denies a young woman the right to a room of her own, the right to pursue her own development as a reader, thinker, and artist, forcing her to surrender this development to the advancement of the male.

In addition, at the structural level Rachel's self-willed death constitutes a refusal of the traditional novel. From beginning to end the narrative can be seen as Rachel's fight with chronological structure. Complexity is found in the constant tension between Rachel's lateral sense of being and the linear force of the ship on its way to a particular destination, the linearity of the trips up and down the mountain and the river, the linear force of Rachel's life on its way to heterosexist coupling. Woolf repeats the traditional story of the female *bildungsroman* that can only end in marriage or death, but her repetition subverts that very tradition. Rachel's death is no accident; rather it issues from her refusal to serve the institutions of male privilege, marriage, and the masculine plot. Concluding a work of art with the death of the heroine—whether it be in *The Mill on the Floss* or *The Voyage Out,* in *Hedda Gabler, The Awakening,* or *The House of Mirth*—need not be a sign of victimization, cynicism or futility. The possibility to refuse the compromise is what makes art such a powerful tool for cultural critique.

In contrast to Rachel and in spite of gender constraints in education and the professions, in spite of incest, pressures to marry, Hyslop's advice and Mitchell's rest cure, Woolf's productive life made major contributions to literary and feminist studies and to the history of ideas. In Woolf's *Letters* there are numerous references to ink, nibs and pens. Elaine Scarry describes how the hand itself may be altered by the pen that endows "the hand with a voice that has more permanence than the speaking voice," and relieves "communication of the requirement that speaker and listener be physically present in the same space.... The natural hand (burnable, breakable, small, and silent) now becomes the artifact-hand (unburnable, unbreakable, large, and endlessly vocal)."[14] Woolf knew the breakable, small, and silent side of her body, and she understood the transformation made possible by a pen in hand that gave her the power of reconstruction. As artist, feminist, and socialist, she did question and challenge the mental health and authority of the doctors, the inquisitors, and the psychiatrists, and through the character of Rachel Vinrace and her voyage out, Woolf condemns a society that continues to restrict women to the narrow confines of marriage and motherhood.

In the Breeches, Petticoats and Pleasures of *Orlando*

> *Meanwhile the indefiniteness remains, and the limits of variation are really much wider than any one would imagine from the sameness of women's coiffure and the favourite love-stories in prose and verse.*
>
> George Eliot
> *Middlemarch*

> *And it is difficult to predict where a shift in the attribution of sexual powers might lead. But the misprisions needed to maintain the established order lead one to suspect that such an operation might take us far.*
>
> Luce Irigaray
> *Speculum*

Published in 1928, *Orlando* was, as Leonard called it, the turning point in Woolf's career as a successful novelist. *To the Lighthouse* had sold 3,873 copies in its first year; *Orlando* sold 8,104 copies in its first six months, earning enthusiastic letters and praise. Money worries were over, and when Woolf went to Cambridge to lecture at Newnham and Girton the same year, there was "an atmosphere of triumph—a kind of ovation."[1]

Orlando's protagonist is a young poet with shapely legs and a handsome body, a transgressive figure who remains amazingly youthful—sixteen on the first page and thirty-six on the last—lives through four centuries and has a sex change halfway through the narrative. In her Diary Woolf wrote that she wanted *Orlando* to be "truthful; but fantastic" and the tone "has to be half laughing, half serious: with great splashes of exaggeration."[2] While fantastic it is, critics usually read the novel as biography or view it as a love letter. However, by lifting *Orlando* out of the particulars of Woolf's life—by refusing to talk about it in those terms—other aspects of this versatile and contraband text materialize. This chapter explores *Orlando*'s revolutionary view of gender, identity, and the body, and the way critical response has tended to quell the rebellion.

Initially for the part of Orlando, Woolf imagined a character who somewhat resembled Lucy Snowe in Charlotte Brontë's *Villette*. Woolf wrote in her diary:

> I sketched the possibilities which an unattractive woman, penniless, alone, might yet bring into being. I began imagining the position—how she would stop a motor on the Dover road, & so get to Dover: cross the channel &c. It struck me, vaguely, that I might write a Defoe narrative for fun.[3]

But Woolf abandoned these initial plans, choosing instead to confer on Orlando beauty, charm, aristocratic lineage, and hereditary wealth. And, to make certain that, in contrast to Lucy Snowe, her protagonist had every advantage, Woolf allowed Orlando to inhabit the first hundred pages as an attractive "boy/man," with all the privilege those words entail. By eliminating the potential problems caused by lack of status, wealth and beauty, Woolf could focus all the more sharply on issues of gender.

Orlando's first sentence begins, "He—for there could be no doubt of his sex, though the fashion of the time did something to disguise it...."[4] Calling the reader's attention immediately to gender, Woolf protests too much, creating the very doubt the words would deny. As J. J. Wilson notes, in the first word Woolf says just what she does not want us to think.[5] Judy Little writes that the narrative's first word announces a masculine subject, yet the male subject "is immediately and comically dismantled by the interruptive qualifications.... The first sentence is what every sentence in the book is about and what every sentence continues to produce and unproduce in rhetorical play."[6] Even when external dress clearly signifies "man" or "woman," the text delights in erotic confusion regarding what "body" is under the garment, how that "body" has come to be, and how it performs. Wild women at Wapping Old Stairs perch on Orlando's knee and fling their arms round his neck, "guessing that something out of the common lay hid beneath his duffel cloak" and "as eager to come at the truth of the matter as Orlando himself" (29).

After serving as treasurer to Queen Elizabeth and as British ambassador to Constantinople and almost midway through the story, Orlando wakes up "a woman" and remains one, more or less, to the novel's end. While the reader may be startled or amused, Orlando remains uninterested in her sex until she decides to sail from Turkey to England and must dress as a "lady." She has been living with the gypsies and wearing Turkish trousers, and Gypsy women "except in one or two important particulars, differ very little from the gipsy men." The narrator comments that it "is a strange fact, but a true one that up to this moment she had scarcely given her sex a thought" (153).

These words—"had scarcely given her sex a thought"—indicate a significant difference between Orlando and the transsexuals and transvestites Marjorie Garber describes in *Vested Interests: Cross-Dressing and Cultural Anxiety*. Garber's transsexuals and transvestites are "*more* concerned with maleness and femaleness than persons who are neither transvestite nor transsexual. They are emphatically not interested in 'unisex' or 'androgyny' as erotic styles, but rather in gender-marked and gender-coded identity structures" [original emphasis].[7] In contrast, Orlando disdains the loss or partialness implicit in a singular gender identity; she refuses the anxious need to clearly define. S/he never feels or suggests "a woman trapped in a man's body" or "a man trapped in the body of a woman." Orlando codes his dress according to practicality and sexual desire.

Clipping the trees, he wears breeches and desiring the love of a woman, he wears the suit of a nobleman. In order to sail for England, Orlando, as a man-changed-into-a-woman who has been wearing Turkish trousers, must dress like a "lady." In this triple configuration the "lady" signifies woman as artifact designed from an assembly of parts. According to the text, Orlando changes to "a complete outfit of such clothes as women then wore, and it was in the dress of a young Englishwoman of rank that she now sat on the deck of the *Enamored Lady*" (153). Such an outfit might include a walking dress with corset and under-skirt edged with ribbon, a linen vest with collar, short jacket belted with a sash, hat with feathers, and parasol and kid gloves. Not only does Orlando feel constrained, but because being "female" and "woman" are contingent and relational performances, men now treat her in radically different ways.

The captain of the ship offers "with the greatest politeness, to have an awning spread for her on deck" and at dinner asks, "A little of the fat, Ma'am?...Let me cut you just the tiniest little slice the size of your finger nail" (155). Orlando remembers that as a young man she insisted that women be obedient, chaste, scented and exquisitely apparelled, and now she will pay in her own person for these desires: "for women are not (judging by my own short experience of the sex) obedient, chaste, scented, and exquisitely apparelled by nature. They can only attain these graces, without which they may enjoy none of the delights of life, by the most tedious discipline" (156–57). The voyage from Turkey allows for an extended satirical treatment of the dress and performance of being female, but upon arrival in England, dress pales in relation to the power of the law to determine identity.

In England Orlando faces three major legal charges: that she is dead, that she is a woman, "which amounts to much the same thing," and that she is an English Duke who has married a dancer and has three sons. Thus, "it was in a highly ambiguous condition, uncertain whether she was alive or dead, man or woman, Duke or nonentity, that she posted down to her country seat" (168). The law's deferral provides Orlando with the liberty to continue to experiment with a variety of costumes and roles, and she occupies numerous gender zones through the course of each day. Each role implies an instance of cross-dressing except that no one role presumes to be the "true" Orlando, the original ground from which she crosses over.

At no other time in the narrative is there so much play and destabilization as during this juridical uncertainty. Knowing both gender codes, Orlando's sex

> changed far more frequently than those who have worn only one set of clothing can conceive; nor can there be any doubt that she reaped a twofold harvest by this device; the pleasures of life were increased and its experiences multiplied. From the probity of breeches she turned to the seductiveness of petticoats and enjoyed the love of both sexes equally. (221)

In the morning, dressed in a China robe of ambiguous gender, she reads her books; in the afternoon in knee breeches she clips the nut trees; in the late afternoon in a flowered taffeta she is off for a drive to

Richmond and a proposal of marriage from some great nobleman; then, in a snuff-colored gown like a lawyer's she visits the courts to hear how her case is doing; and at night, "more often than not," she walks the streets in the black velvet suit of a nobleman (221). Throughout *Orlando* dress is a constant theme, different clothes addressing different desires and sexual relations. Gender becomes a cultural performance shown to be historically, even geographically, contingent and in the service of the regulatory systems of reproduction and compulsory heterosexuality. Anticipating Judith Butler's claim that gender identity is a stylized repetition of acts through time, the novel demonstrates possibilities for gender transformation in the arbitrary relation of these acts and in their subversive repetitions.[8]

One evening Orlando meets the prostitute Nell, and to "feel her hanging lightly yet like a suppliant on her arm" rouses all the feelings that become a man (216–17). Perceiving that Nell's timidity, hesitation, and fumbling are all put on to "gratify her masculinity," Orlando looks, feels, and talks like a man. Still, this meeting between Orlando and Nell represents only a slightly exaggerated version of ordinary relations between "men" and "women." Different types of clothing signal masculinity or femininity and set in motion personal relations of control and submission. When Orlando tells Nell she is a woman, Nell's manner changes quickly, and she immediately drops her plaintive, appealing ways (218).

Orlando's gaming way with clothes, sex, and love repeats itself in other characters such as Harriet/Harry and Sasha. The Archduchess Harriet, six feet high and resembling "nothing so much as a hare," passionately pursues Orlando the man. When Orlando returns from Turkey a woman, the Archduchess Harriet reappears and in the few seconds it takes Orlando to turn to the cupboard and back again, Harriet becomes a man while a "heap of clothes lay in the fender." Alone with a man and recalled "thus suddenly to a consciousness of her sex, which she had [once again] completely forgotten," Orlando feels faint. The Archduke kisses her hand as Orlando sips wine; in short, "they acted the parts of man and woman for ten minutes with great vigour and then fell into natural discourse" (178–79). When Orlando wants something—to sail for England, for example, or the love of a woman, or to be able to write—she plays the parts of "man" or "woman" well, knowing how to make her body legible in either language. Still, at other times "in the robe of ambiguous gender" she appears outside and forgetful of these roles.

When first introduced, Sasha's extraordinary seductive figure, "whether boy's or woman's, for the loose tunic and trousers of the Russian fashion served to disguise the sex," fills Orlando with the "highest curiosity" (37). As in the case of the Archduke's initial attraction to Orlando as a man, the text marks seductiveness as independent of gender; instead, it's the very uncertainty that characters find so seductive. Orlando calls Sasha an olive tree, an emerald, and a fox, metaphors conveying elusiveness and carrying no signs of one gender or the other. When "the boy, for alas, a boy it must be—no woman could skate with such speed and vigour, swept almost on tiptoe past him, Orlando was ready to tear his hair with vexation that the person was of his own sex, and thus all embraces were out of the question." Yet, upon closer examination, "Legs, hands, carriage, were a boy's, but no boy ever had a mouth like that.... She was not a handsbreadth off. She was a woman" (38). These several and sudden shifts create an uncertainty about Sasha that persists as "there was something hidden; in all she did, however daring, there was something concealed" (47). Gender trouble is contagious in *Orlando*, a playful trouble that questions the possibility, need, or advantage of any stable notion of identity.

In terms of both her pleasure and the law, Orlando's sex is still in dispute well into the nineteenth century when, in contrast to her own situation, she observes all round her the necessity for heterosexual coupling where people are

> somehow stuck together, couple after couple.... It did not seem to be Nature.... There was no indissoluble alliance among the brutes that she could see. Could it be Queen Victoria then, or Lord Melbourne? Was it from them that the great discovery of marriage proceeded? Yet the Queen, she pondered, was said to be fond of dogs, and Lord Melbourne, she had heard, was said to be fond of women. It was strange—it was distasteful; indeed, there was something in this indissolubility of bodies which was repugnant to her sense of decency and sanitation. (242)

Historicizing the institution of marriage and condemning it as indecent, Orlando can, for a time, pretend that nothing has changed, "that the climate was the same; that one could still say what one liked and wear knee-breeches or skirts as the fancy took one" (231). In the nineteenth century, nevertheless, things have changed. With her sex still in dispute, without a husband and pregnant, Orlando's naked finger is "sorely afflicted," so afflicted that she cannot write. The spirit of the Victorian Age demands that one wear a wedding ring, and there "was nothing for it but to buy one of those ugly bands and wear it like the rest" (243).

In the midst of all the irreverence and fluidity, Orlando's writing sustains the narrative's one constant fact. Woolf regularly returns to the importance of reading and especially writing—to Orlando's need to write: "The taste for books was an early one. As a child he was sometimes found at midnight by a page still reading. They took his taper away, and he bred glow-worms to serve his purpose. They took the glow-worms away, and he almost burnt the house down with a tinder" (73). He reads voraciously and writes "twenty tragedies and a dozen histories and a score of sonnets" by the time he is eighteen (24). "Never had any boy begged apples as Orlando begged paper; nor sweet meats as he begged ink" (76); and at twenty-five he has written "some forty-seven plays, histories, romances, poems; some in prose, some in verse; some in French, some in Italian" (77). In the nineteenth century in order to continue writing, Orlando must submit and "consider the most desperate of remedies...and take a husband" (243). The crinoline she buys feels

> heavier and more drab than any dress she had yet worn. None had ever so impeded her movements. No longer could she stride through the garden with her dogs, or run lightly to the high mound and fling herself beneath the oak tree. Her skirts collected damp leaves and straw.... The thin shoes were quickly soaked and mudcaked. Her muscles had lost their pliancy. (244–45)

The clothing not only impedes movement but alters the pliancy of the muscles, thus, altering the physical body.

Living as a "Victorian woman," Orlando begins to feel her solitude as loneliness, and rather than "thrusting the gate open, she tapped with a gloved hand for the porter to unfasten it for her" (247). Rather than striding through the park, she becomes fearful and apprehensive lest some animal or man attack her. Thus, the socio-cultural climate shapes her body, dress, and personality as well. In wearing the Victorian costume and in marrying, Orlando performs a deep obeisance to the spirit of the age, and "she heaved a deep sigh of relief, as, indeed, well she might, for the transaction between a writer and the spirit of the age is one of infinite delicacy.... Now, therefore, she could write, and write she did. She wrote. She wrote. She wrote" (266).

However, even after Orlando meets her husband Shelmerdine, gender trouble persists and prospers. "An awful suspicion rushed into both their minds simultaneously. 'You're a woman, Shel!... You're a man, Orlando!'" (252). And is Orlando really married? If her husband is always sailing around the Horn in the teeth of a gale, if she likes him, if she likes other people, and, finally, if she still wants more than anything to write poetry, is it marriage? "She had her doubts" (264). Under all the signs of conformity—a legal pronouncement, a wedding ring, a crinoline—Orlando feels something else, something "highly contraband" that if clearly visible would cause her to "pay the full fine. She had only escaped by the skin of her teeth" (265–66). In comparison to romance plots, the events leading to Orlando's marriage—she becomes pregnant before she meets Shel, she marries in order to write, she considers it the most desperate of remedies—are highly irregular. When Orlando turns into Hyde Park, several park keepers look at her with suspicion and are "only brought to a favourable opinion of her sanity by noticing the pearl necklace which she wore" (284). Like the marriage certificate and ring, the pearl necklace functions as a sign of respectability, capable of overcoming other threatening signs and transforming suspicion and distrust into acceptance.

In spite of the persistent gender trouble in *Orlando*, in the critical conversations surrounding the novel there is a tendency toward what Garber calls an "*underestimation* of the object," "a tendency to erase the third term, to appropriate the cross-dresser 'as' one of two sexes."[9] Garber herself is guilty of this tendency, this underestimation of the object, in her discussion of *Orlando*. In her brief treatment, she writes, "Whatever Orlando *is,* her clothing reflects it: the crossing between male and female may be a mixture (a synthesis), but it is not a confusion, a transgression. The inside always corresponds to the outside."[10] Garber bases her interpretation on the following comment: "Clothes are but a symbol of something hid deep beneath. It was a change in Orlando herself that dictated her choice of a woman's dress and a woman's sex" (188). However, the text immediately corrects this simplistic view:

> For here again, we come to a dilemma. Different though the sexes are, they intermix. In every human being a vacillation from one sex to the other takes place, and often it is only the clothes that keep the male or female likeness, which underneath the sex is the very opposite of what it is above. Of the complications and confusions which thus result every one has had experience.... (189)

On the preceding page the text reads: "there is much to support the view that it is clothes that wear us and not we them; we may make them take the mould of arm or breast, but they mould our hearts, our brains, our tongues to their liking." Clearly, the entire passage to which these quotes belong represents conflicting points of view, and our experience of "complications and confusions" is the point.

In discussing this "famous androgynous statement," Pamela L. Caughie writes that it is often taken out of context and cited as unambiguous truth: "The androgynous Orlando is appropriated as a symbol of the more unified self, or as a resolution to the problem of true self and conventional self. 'Androgynous wholeness' is the phrase Sandra Gilbert uses." Caughie argues instead that in the midst of the text's violent shifts in viewpoint, Woolf's androgynous statement is "a way to remain suspended between opposed beliefs," that *Orlando* not only questions conventional assumptions regarding sexuality but also conventional assumptions about language itself, challenging the reference theory of meaning.[11] Clothing, identity, and rhetoric are not "an ornamentation of something prior, but an orientation to something else. What matters is not what they mask or mark, but what they enable the protagonist or the writer to accomplish."[12] Herein lies the principle difference between Garber's psychoanalytic focus on absence and lack and Woolf's emphasis in *Orlando* on transvestitism as subversive repetition, a practice and performance of rich possibilities and satisfied desires. *Orlando* offers a critique of binary sex and gender distinctions, calling into question the whole notion of "inside"—core identity—essentialism, and

> it is not because it simply makes such distinctions reversible but because it denaturalizes...signs. When a homosexual relation seems to trope off a

heterosexual relation, what is revealed is that the signs by which heterosexuality had encoded and recognized itself have been detached from a referent with which those signs are thereby revealed to have had a conventional rather than natural connection.[13]

Cross-dressed as a nobleman, Orlando courts Nell the prostitute, and their relation mimics—"tropes off" in Garber's words—the heterosexual relation between the Captain of the *Enamoured Lady* and Orlando dressed as a "lady." Orlando uses identity as a practice and performance, disrupting not only the categories of male and female, but the concept of category itself.[14]

Orlando, as Makiko Minow-Pinkney claims, is perhaps the most neglected of Woolf's novels.[15] Frequently, when *Orlando* does receive attention, it is reduced to therapy, a "love letter" or tribute to Vita Sackville-West. Like pearls and marriage certificates, signs like "therapy," "love letter," and "tribute" can be read conventionally and "understood." Jean O. Love writes that whereas *To the Lighthouse* transcends particulars, *Orlando* is not quite able to do so: "In fact, it cannot be completely understood outside the context of her friendship with Vita Sackville-West.... It is best read, I think, as her ultimate comment on Vita and as her means of gaining perspective and detachment in order to continue their friendship on a different basis."[16] According to Quentin Bell, *Orlando* "is interesting biographically, partly because it commemorates Virginia's love for Vita, and partly because we can trace so many of its elements to the incidents of Virginia's daily life in those years," and he comments, "I think that she saw well enough that *Orlando* was not 'important' among her works."[17] Nigel Nicolson calls *Orlando* "the longest and most charming love letter in literature" (202), and this reduction appears on the book cover, creating expectations in the reader.[18] Mitchell A. Leaska explains his omission of *Orlando* from *The Novels of Virginia Woolf* by writing: "to have included a discussion of that brilliant but incongruous piece of phantasy between these covers would have been tantamount to committing a violation of literary kinship."[19] Recognizing these common pitfalls in reading *Orlando*, Wilson writes that it is too easily dismissed as a *jeu d'esprit* or is taken too seriously, and she warns the reader to remain alert to *Orlando*'s "subversive motives."[20]

While I do not mean to diminish the importance of Vita Sackville-West in Woolf's life or writing, the omission of *Orlando* from critical discussions because it is presumed to be a "biography" or is reduced to an escapade or "love letter" works to silence this radical text. If the point of *Orlando* is reduced to the author's attempts at self-help or her relation to Vita, its subversion becomes a subversion of little social and political importance. This single-minded attention to two people rather than to the legal and political construction of the body dismisses or reduces to a ghostly presence Orlando's radical sexual transgressions wherein "the pleasures of life were increased and its experiences multiplied" (221).

Elizabeth Meese celebrates *Orlando* as a lesbian "love affair of the letter," writing, "Virginia sees, first and foremost, a lesbian, and invests in Vita, through the character of Orlando, the history of women 'like' her...."[21] To mark and own the text in this way would be an exclusionary move, curtailing the text and denying access to others, to the non-lesbian, homosexual, heterosexual, or bisexual. Sherron E. Knopp comments, "*Orlando* is obviously not about the sapphic love of Vita and Virginia, even in a disguised way. The hero/heroine loves men and women over the course of four hundred years, but no one of these is the subject."[22] One way to reinscribe a text into dominant culture is to rewrite it in critical conversations by reducing it to particulars, to the personal and romantic, to biography or therapy, to a certain gender ontology, for example. To contain or restrict a radical text like *Orlando* is to discount its effect and prevent it from influencing and altering other texts and other discourses.

Rachel Blau DuPlessis writes about Orlando and Shel that "Androgynous characters cannot be assigned stable places in hierarchies of gender status, nor do they even adhere to physical norms: Shel is both dainty and brawny, for example."[23] Caughie writes that *Orlando* expresses "the difficulty of reaching conclusions about identity or language," but Caughie, like DuPlessis, retains the word "androgyny," defining it as "a refusal to choose." Yet, the rest of this sentence might read: "a refusal to choose between male and female." Caughie writes that one "must assume a sexual identity in order to take one's place in language, in order to express anything. Sexual identity is assumed in language."[24] Sexual identity is assumed in language as known, but language is not universal or unchanging. Caughie's point could just as well be a question. How do we alter language and the other ways we make ourselves legible, like dress, to transform identity politics into a liberatory practice and performance?

"Androgyny" presupposes male and female: in the word's definition—"having the characteristics or nature of both male and female"—androgyny continues to hold fast to and maintain the very binary system it would seem to escape. In the writing of Meese, DuPlessis, and Caughie, one senses *Orlando*'s dissolution of boundaries and subsequent excess. Still, words like "androgynous," "lesbian," "bisexual," and "ambisexual" continue to function within a binary frame and always recall male and female, A and not-A, "dainty and brawny." While Woolf herself sometimes discusses Orlando in these terms—"this mixture in her of man and woman" (189)—I argue that Orlando's story that began as a joke and became serious moves beyond and in excess of the narrator's or Woolf's understanding. Garber writes, "Even if we possess documentary 'evidence' that an artist has a certain 'meaning' in mind, the unconscious of the text...may be in conflict with the conscious purpose of its maker.... [T]he two sets of intentions might well be expected to come into conflict with one another."[25] Rosemary Jackson writes that "fantasy characteristically attempts to compensate for a lack resulting from cultural constraints: it is a literature of desire, which seeks that which is experienced as absence and loss."[26] The desire in the case of *Orlando*, as Minow-Pinkney maintains, "is so radical that it was immediately repressed by the author herself as a 'joke,' and has subsequently been dismissed (i.e. repressed) by critics as non-essential."[27] To end sexual polarization, it is necessary to refuse labels and their corresponding restraints and exclusions; it is necessary to free ourselves from the internal paradox of foundationalism that "presumes, fixes, and constrains the very 'subjects' that it hopes to represent and liberate."[28]

Six days before the publication of *Orlando*, Woolf went to court prepared to testify in behalf of another subversive text. Radclyffe Hall's *The Well of Loneliness* had been seized by the police, and at the hearing the magistrate found the novel to be obscene, ordered the seized copies destroyed, and fined the publisher and bookseller.[29] In "Below the Belt: (Un)Covering *The Well of Loneliness*," Michèle Aina Barale examines four different book covers of *The Well of Loneliness* to explain how dominant culture makes marginalized texts read as its own. Referring to book covers as "textual garments," Barale writes that covers "fashion" how we perceive the text and like "all clothing, these garments reveal some parts and conceal others."[30] While initially *The Well of Loneliness* was seized and condemned, Barale's point is that even after numerous editions and reprints, the narrative continues to be appropriated by dominant culture to enhance heterosexual desire. I am suggesting that a similar appropriation, achieved through packaging, labeling and critical naming, has rendered *Orlando*'s subversion nearly invisible.

Woolf wrote about *Orlando*, "L. takes *Orlando* more seriously than I had expected. Thinks it in some ways better than the *Lighthouse:* about more interesting things, and with more attachment to life and larger. The truth is I expect I began it as a joke and went on with it seriously."[31] As a literary work, the novel breaks with tradition in substantial ways, transgressing literary laws not only in the person of the protagonist but also in the novel's form and style, fantastic plot and elaborate diction. Susan M. Squier writes that in terms of character, Woolf inverted all the techniques of formal realism in order not to focus on identity, but to call it into question.[32] Toril Moi claims that Woolf was sixty years in advance of Julia Kristeva in calling for the deconstruction of the opposition between masculinity and femininity and challenging the very notion of identity.[33] Because Orlando lives through centuries, defies labels, and loves both men and women, it is impossible to define or identify with him/her in any traditional way.

As a consequence of the discourse of sexuality, certain areas of the body will signify eroticism, embarrassment, shame, or power. This is sexuality not as a natural given that power tries to hold in check, but sexuality as "an especially dense transfer point for relations of power."[34] Although we are taught to read physical features as existing outside of language in a presocial ontology, through a process of repeated naming, gender identity produces and naturalizes itself in symbolic structures of anatomy. As we grow, we are conditioned to see and understand bodies in specific and political ways. Being "female" is not a natural fact, but a cultural code and performance, a repeated stylization of the body that congeals over time and produces the appearance of substance, of a natural being.[35] The question "Is it a boy or a girl"? is only the beginning of a process requiring hard work and incessant attention.

The idea that subjectivity is the effect of external circumstance is a serious matter, but as Butler points out, "laughter in the face of serious categories is indispensable for feminism. Without a doubt, feminism continues to require its own forms of serious play."[36] Laughter changes the face and the body, has its own sounds, and creates a distance from the object of amusement or ridicule. With laughter, the tone changes, undermining and diminishing the formidability of what is being laughed at. These changes in the body, tone, and location alter the relation; there is an exchange of power in laughter, and laughter is one way to take control. Humor is aggressive in its direct confrontation with dominant forces, and in *Orlando* Woolf laughs in the face of the law, the "natural" body, codes of dress and behavior, and romantic love. Over and over the text mocks its own pursuit of Orlando, its own attempt to pin him down, to know the biographical facts of her life and define her essential person. The text marks subjectivity as multiple and shifting, and any attempt to define Orlando's identity is useless. Through laughter Woolf subversively repeats and ridicules convention and suggests the possibility of refusing an essentialist and binary mode of thinking. Through *Orlando*'s pleasures and laughter, Woolf creates another location from which to evaluate and participate in the social construction of gender, body, and desire.

Epilogue

Before writing *Jane Eyre* in 1846, Charlotte Brontë told her sisters that "they were wrong—even morally wrong—in making their heroines beautiful as a matter of course. They replied that it was impossible to make a heroine interesting on any other terms." Accepting their challenge, Charlotte replied, "I will prove to you that you are wrong; I will show you a heroine as plain and as small as myself, who shall be as interesting as any of yours."[1] The immediate success of Jane's unattractive little body and strong voice extended an invitation to other authors to capture in literary space more of the diversity of women's physical appearance and experience and more of their power, intelligence and passion. As well as seeing the publication of *Jane Eyre* as the feminist moment in the West of "female access to individualism," as Gayatri Spivak views it, the moment can also be distinguished in terms of access to female difference and agency.[2]

Several contemporary critics acknowledge the power of the novel to shape culture, but they argue that novels, especially those of the nineteenth century, produced and perpetuated the middle class. More specifically, they maintain that novels produced and enforced female domesticity and bourgeois subjectivity. In *Desire and Domestic Fiction,* Nancy Armstrong assumes some kind of agency when she locates in *Pamela*, other novels, and conduct books a domestic woman—a body filled with self-regulation, modesty, vigilance, and a spotless soul—arising as a reaction, a dialectical response, to the aristocratic woman.[3] Yet, the dialectical process that Armstrong identifies should not be restricted to producing only a domestic subject. Novels possess the power to respond in other subversive ways to both aristocratic and domestic configurations of femininity.

In *Other Women: The Writing of Class, Race, and Gender, 1832–1898*, Anita Levy dissolves generic differences, writing that "fiction is no less true than science." Levy locates a good deal of agency in fictional representation, arguing that the human sciences and fiction in Britain between 1840 and 1890 produced a "natural" female figure which in turn brought about the middle-class revolution and the formation of the modern political state.[4] Yet, Levy leaves little space for distinctions among a very large and diverse group of authors. Several times she refers specifically to the "intellectual labor of women" as a socializing practice, but never as a practice that resisted and ran counter to the status quo.

Dombey and Son (1847) and *The Mill on the Floss* (1860) are examples of novels frequently categorized together as Victorian, and at several points they intersect structurally and thematically. Throughout Eliot's *Letters*, there are nearly one hundred references to Dickens, and she had read many if not all of his novels. Their personal friendship and her familiarity with his work as well as the similarities between the novels suggest that in creating Maggie Tulliver, Eliot may have been responding directly to *Dombey and Son*. When these two novels are juxtaposed, one is struck by the way the active and passionate Maggie Tulliver appears as a subversive repetition of the lifeless ideal embodied in Florence Dombey.[5] Levy and I agree on the "very power of fiction" to bring about change; where we disagree is in the assessment of the diverse effects of that power.

In *A Literature of Their Own* Elaine Showalter identifies three stages which women writers have experienced: imitation, protest, and self-discovery, labeling these stages feminine, feminist, and female respectively. In the first stage women imitated prevailing modes of the dominant tradition and internalized its standards of art and its views on social roles, and Showalter marks the end of the first feminine stage with the death of George Eliot in 1880.[6] Showalter writes that the categories are not rigid, that there are feminist elements in feminine writing, and that one may find all three stages in the career of a single author. Still, this kind of linear progressive approach fails to address the complexity of novelistic discourse and fails to acknowledge an author's need to negotiate with the spirit of her own historical period. "New currents in behavioral ideology," according to Volosinov, "no matter how revolutionary they may be, undergo the influence of the established ideological systems, and, to some extent, incorporate forms, ideological practices, and approaches already in stock."[7] Male pseudonyms signify only one of the strategies Brontë and Eliot employed in order to be heard and win widespread support and recognition.

Like Showalter, Rachel Blau DuPlessis constructs her story of women writers as a story of origins wherein postromantic strategies begin with the publication of Olive Schreiner's *The Story of an African Farm* in 1883, explaining that Schreiner "breaks the sentence" so that alternative and oppositional stories about women, men, and community can be constructed beyond the teleological formulations of quest and romance.[8] Yet, there is a long tradition of protest and opposition in novels by women before Showalter's date of 1880 and DuPlessis's date of 1883.

Rather than limit all nineteenth-century fiction to similar aims and effects, rather than find the same "woman" in the sciences and in fiction, throughout this book I have contrasted images of women in religious, legal, and medical discourse with the reconstructions I locate in Brontë, Eliot, and Woolf to demonstrate the significant differences these authors were representing in fictional space. As sites of describable change in a larger historical process, the novels discussed indicate the positive socio-political importance of novels in the larger picture of history and cultural studies. While many prominent critics often view novels as instruments that work to reproduce women in subordinate and exploitive situations, emphasizing women's passivity and victimization, I have argued for a more inclusive view, identifying a different kind of discursive agency in novelistic discourse before 1880.

Because Brontë, Eliot and Woolf are major literary figures, there is an abundance of biographical material which tells much of the story of their relationship to discourse. Understanding that power and knowledge are joined in discourse and that power renders the body active and productive, this book has discussed the ways these three authors experienced in their personal lives and captured in their novels the pleasure and value of reading. A "scene of reading" captures the special significance of the interaction between women and discourse that occurs during such contact. Whether it is Brontë studying in Brussels, Eliot reading German higher criticism, or Woolf in her father's library, such scenes provide the ability to comprehend and alter harmful beliefs and situations and make other choices. By reading numerous books in various disciplines, the reader comes to question any one point of view and to recognize that knowledge is a struggle and that generating persuasive discourse is power. Through reading widely, these authors engaged in a process of making contact with diverse points of view, selecting among contradictory descriptions, definitions and categories, and forming new and distinctive combinations.

In their narratives Brontë, Eliot and Woolf repeated their personal experiences with reading and discourse, expanding the possibilities and forms of everyday life for their female heroines. Jane Eyre's ability to say "no" and her power to move to distant locations allow her the opportunity to reinvent herself, changing her appearance and enlarging her powers of observation and analysis. In spite of difficult circumstances, Lucy Snowe creates a professional career in a foreign country, becoming fluent in French, owning her own school, and narrating her own story. After being rejected by an entire community for her refusal to marry Stephen Guest, the passionate and intelligent Maggie Tulliver dies a heroic death attempting to save her brother. The gifted pianist Rachel Vinrace also dies, choosing death as her only avenue of escape from the narrow confines of marriage and motherhood. The fantastic Orlando, a subject greater than a "man" or a "woman," lives through centuries, displaying the significance of movement and dress in constructing and performing sex and gender. All of these characters are avid readers, and the reading is marked as decisive in determining the choices they make. The novels often comment on the odd and serendipitous ways the characters obtain books and the settings and effects of their reading. Specific book titles frequently appear, and these instances of intertextuality illuminate the way the psyche establishes vital contact with and assimilates diverse ideas and perspectives.

Rather than repetition constrained by the injunction to reconsolidate reductive views of women, Brontë, Eliot and Woolf enact subversive repetitions in their novels, disrupting literary conventions and social scripts and bringing culturally unintelligible bodies into the realm of intelligibility. In this process the female body—often constructed as sinful, weak and dependent—is reconstructed as multiple and diverse bodies, forceful, intelligent and strong. The heroines cast a suspicious eye on the old romance plot, creating in its place a larger imaginary field in which to intervene in the practices of patriarchal culture and represent the vast differences among women. Through the lives of the writers and their heroines, this study narrates an oft repeated journey, beginning with silence, isolation and sometimes abuse and leading through scenes of reading to locations of resistance, intervention and agency. Such a journey from silence to creative change reveals the important role women must perform in all discursive arenas—science, religion and the law as well as literature—in order to generate images of women which cultivate and expand the rich potential of our lives.

Notes

INTRODUCTION:
WOMEN AND THE NOVEL

1. Londa Schiebinger, "Skeletons in the Closet: The First Illustrations of the Female Skeleton in Eighteenth-Century Anatomy," in *The Making of the Modern Body: Sexuality and Society in the Nineteenth Century*, ed. Catherine Gallagher and Thomas Laqueur (Berkeley: University of California Press, 1987), p. 43.

2. Ibid., p. 58.

3. Thomas Laqueur, "Orgasm, Generation, and the Politics of Reproductive Biology," in *The Making of the Modern Body: Sexuality and Society in the Nineteenth Century*, ed. Catherine Gallagher and Thomas Laqueur (Berkeley: University of California Press, 1987), pp. 3–4.

4. Withers Moore, "The Higher Education of Women," *British Medical Journal* (14 August 1886), pp. 296, 297.

5. Ian Watt, *The Rise of the Novel: Studies in Defoe, Richardson and Fielding* (London: Chatto & Windus, 1957), p. 298; and Elaine Showalter, *A Literature of Their Own: British Women Novelists From Brontë to Lessing* (Princeton: Princeton University Press, 1977), p. 13. Dale Spender notes that Watt's statement "The majority of eighteenth century novels were actually by women" is followed by no discussion of these novels. There are no entries in Watt's index or any explanation for the omission. Dale Spender, *Mothers of the Novel: 100 Good Women Writers Before Jane Austen* (London: Pandora, 1986), p. 139.

6. Spender, *Mothers of the Novel*, pp. 117, 3–4.

7. Michel Foucault, *The History of Sexuality: An Introduction*, trans. Robert Hurley (New York: Random House, 1978), pp. 100–101.

8. Judith Butler, *Gender Trouble: Feminism and the Subversion of Identity* (New York: Routledge, 1990), p. 145.

9. Ibid., p. 30.

10. Foucault, *History of Sexuality*, pp. 127, 103, 157.

11. Butler, *Gender Trouble*, p. 7.
12. Matthews Duncan, President's Address, quoted in "Political and Educational Aspects of Obstetric Medicine," *British Medical Journal* (12 March 1881), p. 395.
13. Mary Poovey, *Uneven Developments: The Ideological Work of Gender in Mid-Victorian England* (Chicago: University of Chicago Press, 1988), p. 19.
14. Butler, *Gender Trouble*, p. 146.
15. Joan W. Scott, "The Evidence of Experience," *Critical Inquiry* 17 (summer 1991) pp. 779–80.
16. Ibid., p. 793.

CHAPTER ONE
THE GERMAN CONNECTION IN GEORGE ELIOT

1. Gordon S. Haight, *George Eliot: A Biography* (New York: Penguin, 1968), p. 25.
2. George Eliot, *The George Eliot Letters*, ed. Gordon S. Haight, 9 vols. (New Haven: Yale University Press, 1955–78), 1:23. Subsequent references to this edition will be included parenthetically in the text.
3. William Baker, "New George Eliot Letters," *The George Eliot Review* 23 (1992), p. 33.
4. Thomas Deegan, "Tractatus Theologico-Politicus," *George Eliot—George Henry Lewes Studies* 22–23 (1993), p. 4; Elizabeth Ermarth, *George Eliot* (Boston: Twayne Publishers, 1985), pp. 34–38.
5. Haight, *George Eliot: A Biography* , pp. 172–73.
6. William Baker, *The George Eliot—George Henry Lewes Library: An Annotated Catalogue of Their Books at Dr. Williams's Library, London* (New York: Garland, 1977), p. xxviii.
7. Horton Harris, *David Friedrich Strauss and His Theology* (Cambridge: Cambridge University Press, 1973), p. 41.
8. Marilyn Chapin Massey, *Christ Unmasked: The Meanings of the Life of Jesus in German Politics* (Chapel Hill: University of North Carolina Press, 1983), p. 3.
9. Ibid., p. 47.
10. Ibid., pp. 78–79.
11. *Daily News*, 3 January 1868, p. 4, col. 3.
12. Karl Barth, "An Introductory Essay," in *The Essence of Christianity*, trans. George Eliot (New York: Harper and Row, 1957), p. xi.
13. Ludwig Feuerbach, *The Essence of Christianity*, p. xxxiv.

14. Ibid., p. 83.

15. Friedrich Engels and Karl Marx, "Manifesto of the Communist Party," in *The Marx-Engels Reader*, ed. Robert C. Tucker (New York: W. W. Norton, 1978), p. 477. Subsequent references to this edition will be included parenthetically in the text.

16. George Eliot, *Middlemarch*, ed. David R. Carroll (Oxford: Clarendon, 1986), pp. 384–88.

17. Haight, *George Eliot: A Biography*, p. 99.

18. Feuerbach, *The Essence of Christianity*, pp. 185, 216, 257, 252, 260.

19. George Eliot, *The Mill on the Floss*, ed. Gordon S. Haight (Oxford: Clarendon, 1986), pp. 254–55.

20. Ibid., pp. 219, 221, 220.

21. Feuerbach, *The Essence of Christianity*, pp. 185–86.

22. George Eliot, "The Natural History of German Life," in *Selected Essays, Poems and Other Writings*, ed. A. S. Byatt and Nicholas Warren (New York: Penguin, 1990), pp. 110, 128.

23. Eliot, "William Lecky's *The Influence of Rationalism*," in *Selected Essays*, p. 393.

24. Although written in 1845–46, "The German Ideology" was not published until 1932.

25. Byatt, introduction to *Selected Essays*, p. xi.

26. Leonard Huxley, *Life and Letters of Thomas Henry Huxley* (New York: D. Appleton, 1900), pp. 19–20.

27. *Daily News*, 3 January 1868, p. 4, col. 3.

28. Eliot, "The Natural History of German Life," in *Selected Essays*, pp. 129–30.

29. William Hale White, *Athenæum* (November 28, 1885), quoted in *The George Eliot Letters*, 1:xv–xvi.

30. Eliot, "Address to Working Men, By Felix Holt," in *Essays of George Eliot*, ed. Thomas Pinney (London: Routledge & Kegan Paul, 1963), p. 421.

31. Ibid., p. 425.

32. Haight, *George Eliot: A Biography*, p. 395.

33. Bernard Semmel, *George Eliot and the Politics of National Inheritance* (New York: Oxford University Press, 1994).

34. Eliot, "Margaret Fuller and Mary Wollstonecraft," in *Selected Essays*, p. 335.

CHAPTER TWO
READING MAGGIE READING

1. Kristin Brady, *George Eliot* (New York: St. Martin's Press, 1992), pp. 16, 7.

2. Ibid., p. 18.

3. Sandra M. Gilbert and Susan Gubar, *The Madwoman in the Attic: The Woman Writer and the Nineteenth-Century Literary Imagination* (New Haven: Yale University Press, 1979), pp. 476–77.

4. Nina Auerbach, "The Power of Hunger: Demonism and Maggie Tulliver," *Nineteenth-Century Fiction* 30 (1975), p. 171.

5. Susan Fraiman, "*The Mill on the Floss*, the Critics, and the *Bildungsroman*," *PMLA* 108 (1993), p. 138.

6. See Margaret Homans, "Eliot, Wordsworth, and the Scenes of the Sisters' Instruction," *Critical Inquiry* 8.2 (1981): 223–242; Mary Jacobus, "The Question of Language: Men of Maxims and *The Mill on the Floss*," *Critical Inquiry* 8.2 (1981): 207–222; and Nancy K. Miller, "Emphasis Added: Plots and Plausibilities in Women's Fiction," *PMLA* 96 (1981): 36–48.

7. George Eliot, *The Mill on the Floss* (Oxford: Clarendon, 1980), p. 14. Subsequent references to this edition will be included parenthetically in the text.

8. *The History of the Devil* was first published in 1726, reprinted in 1727, 1734 and 1739 with at least eight more editions appearing in England during the eighteenth century. Two French translations and at least two German editions were published during the eighteenth century. During the nineteenth century the book was regularly reprinted, with many editions appearing in America. In 1744 the Catholic Church placed the book on the *Index of Prohibited Books* most directly because of Defoe's frequent references to the pope as the "Whore of Babylon." Daniel Defoe, *The History of the Devil: Ancient and Modern in Two Parts* (Yorkshire: EP Publishing Limited, 1972). Subsequent references to this edition will be included parenthetically in the text.

9. Jeffrey Russell, *A History of Witchcraft: Sorcerers, Heretics and Pagans* (London: Thames and Hudson, 1980), p. 133.

10. Walter Scott, *Letters on Demonology and Witchcraft* (East Ardsley, Wakefield, England: S. R. Publishers, 1968), p. 320.

11. George Eliot, "The Influence of Rationalism," in *Selected Essays, Poems and Other Writings*, ed. A. S. Byatt and Nicholas Warren (London: Penguin, 1990), pp. 394–95.

12. Even before the Judaeo-Christian monotheistic tradition expelled the feminine principle from the Deity, however, the social position of women was clearly inferior in polytheistic religions. Christianity's chief competitor in the early Roman Empire, Mithraism, denied women salvation and even entry into the temple. Russell, *A History of Witchcraft*, p. 116.

13. "You shall not permit a sorceress to live." Exodus 22:18. RSV. "A man or a

woman who is a medium or a wizard shall be put to death; they shall be stoned with stones, their blood shall be upon them." Leviticus 20:27. RSV. "There shall not be found among you any one...who practices divination, a soothsayer, or an augur, or a sorcerer, or a charmer, or a medium, or a wizard, or a necromancer. For whoever does these things is an abomination to the LORD; and because of these abominable practices the LORD your God is driving them out before you." Deuteronomy 18:10–12. RSV.

14. Anne Llewellyn Barstow, *Witchcraze: A New History of the European Witch Hunts* (San Francisco: Pandora, 1994), p. 26.

15. Barbara Ehrenreich and Deirdre English, *Witches, Midwives, and Nurses: A History of Women Healers* (New York: The Feminist Press, 1973), p. 12.

16. Russell, *A History of Witchcraft*, p. 113.

17. Barstow, *Witchcraze*, p. 113.

18. Six editions of *The Malleus Maleficarum* were printed before 1500, at least fourteen by 1520, and another sixteen by 1669. The text was translated into German, French, Italian, and English, was quoted extensively in later manuals, and quickly spread into civil law. Portions of it were printed in a book belonging to Increase Mather, and it likely helped in spreading the witchcraze to New England. Barstow, *Witchcraze*, p. 171. The text concludes with an official letter of approbation from the theological faculty of the University of Cologne. In his introduction to the 1948 edition, Montague Summers refers to *The Malleus* as the "most important, wisest, and weightiest books of the world," and says that it "is a work which must irresistibly capture the attention of all men who think, all who see, or are endeavouring to see, the ultimate reality beyond the accidents of matter, time and space." Heinrich Krämer and James Sprenger, *The Malleus Maleficarum*, trans. Montague Summers (London, 1928; New York: Dover Publication, 1971), pp. viii, x.

19. Ibid., pp. 43, 44.

20. Eliot, "The Influence of Rationalism," in *Selected Essays*, p. 395.

21. Another how-to manual "The Discovery of Witches" compiled in 1612 states, "And these the Devils marks...be often in their secretest parts, and therefore require diligent and careful search." C. L'Estrange Ewen, *Witchcraft and Demonianism* (London: Heath Cranton Limited, 1933), p. 267. Women's genitals were routinely searched, and at a 1593 witch trial an investigator, discovering the woman's clitoris, identified it as the devil's teat; he "meant not to disclose, because it was adjoining to so secret a place which was not decent to be seen; yet in the end, not willing to conceal so strange a matter," he showed it to the others. The woman was convicted. Barbara Rosen, *Witchcraft* (New York: Taplinger, 1972), pp. 296–97.

22. Ilza Veith, *Hysteria, The History of a Disease* (Chicago: University of Chicago Press, 1965), p. 60.

23. Ehrenreich and English, *Witches, Midwives, and Nurses*, p. 6.

24. Often, a rope was tied around the suspected witch's body, and the rope supported her in such a way that it was entirely dependent upon the two men holding its ends whether she sank or not. Documents taken from the Public Record Office 1612 give instructions for administering this test: "Binding their armes crosse...throw them into the water, yet least they should not bee witches, and that their liues might not be in danger of drowning, let there be a roape tyed about their middles, so long that it may reach from one side of your damme to the other, where on each side let one of your men stand, that if she chance to sinke they may draw her up and preserve her. Then if she swimme, take her up and cause some women to search her, upon which if they find any extraordinarie markes about her, let her the second time be bound, and have her right thumbe bound to her left toe, and her left thumbe to her right toe, and your men with the same rope (if need be) to preserve her, and bee throwne into the water when if she swimme, you may build upon it, that she is a witch, I have seen it often tried in the North countrey." Ewen, *Witchcraft and Demonianism*, pp. 206, 205.

25. Eliot's essay "Woman in France: Madam de Sablé" begins: "In 1847, a certain Count Leopold Ferri died at Padua, leaving a library entirely composed of works written by women, in various languages, and this library amounted to nearly 32,000 volumes." *Selected Essays*, p. 8.

26. There are 700 surviving manuscripts of *The Imitation of Christ*, twenty-two dated before 1441. The first printed edition appeared in 1471, the year Thomas à Kempis died, and there have been 6,000 subsequent editions. Only the Bible has been translated into more languages. Thomas à Kempis, *The Imitation of Christ*, ed. Ernest Rhys (London: J. M. Dent, 1910). Subsequent references to this edition will be included parenthetically in the text.

27. George Eliot had read Thomas à Kempis on at least three occasions. The first time was in 1849 when she served constantly at her father's deathbed. In February of this year she wrote to Sara Hennell: "I have at last the most delightful 'de imitatione Christi' with quaint woodcuts. One breathes a cool air as of cloisters in the book—it makes one long to be a saint for a few months" (*Letters* 1:278). Although she gave this copy to Sara Hennell in January of 1851, Haight notes that a few months later she was again reading *De Imitatione Christi* while romantically entangled with John Chapman, his wife Elisabeth, and his mistress Susanna. The third time Eliot went to Thomas à Kempis was while writing *The Mill on the Floss*. According to Haight, the first mention of the novel occurs in a journal entry dated January 12, 1859 (*George Eliot, A*

Biography, p. 302). On November 18, 1859 Eliot closes a journal entry with " I am reading Thomas à Kempis" (*Letters* 3:205), and the following March, she finished the novel.

28. In Chapter VII the narrator writes, "Certainly the contrast between the cousins was conspicuous, and, to superficial eyes, was very much to the disadvantage of Maggie, though a connoisseur might have seen 'points' in her which had a higher promise for maturity than Lucy's natty completeness. It was like the contrast between a rough, dark, overgrown puppy and a white kitten." *The Mill on the Floss*, p. 53.

29. According to a translator's note, Corinne is named after a Greek woman well known for her lyric poetry with whom Pindar had studied. Madame de Staël published the novel in 1807, and it was an immediate success, exerting a substantial and far-reaching influence, particularly on literary women. Madame de Staël, *Corinne or Italy*, trans. Avriel H. Goldberger (New Brunswick: Rutgers University Press, 1987), p. 257. Subsequent references to this edition will be included parenthetically in the text.

30. Deborah Heller, "Tragedy, Sisterhood, and Revenge in *Corinne*," *Papers on Language and Literature: A Journal for Scholars and Critics of Language and Literature* 26.2 (1990), pp. 215, 218.

31. Madelyn Gutwirth, "Woman as Mediatrix: From Jean-Jacques Rousseau to Germaine de Staël," in *Woman as Mediatrix: Essays on Nineteenth-Century European Women Writers*, ed. Avriel H. Goldberger (New York: Greenwood Press, 1987), p. 21.

32. Jacobus, "The Question of Language," p. 216.

CHAPTER THREE
VOICE AND VISIBILITY IN CHARLOTTE BRONTË

1. Carole Pateman, *The Sexual Contract* (Stanford: Stanford University Press, 1988), p. 90.

2. Sally Shuttleworth, *Charlotte Brontë and Victorian Psychology* (Cambridge: Cambridge University Press, 1996), pp. 2–3, 244.

3. Gayatri Spivak, "Three Women's Texts and a Critique of Imperialism," in *"Race" Writing, and Difference*, ed. Henry Louis Gates, Jr. (Chicago: University of Chicago Press, 1985); Nancy Armstrong and Leonard Tennenhouse, "Introduction: Representing Violence, or 'How the West Was Won,'" in *The Violence of Representation: Literature and the History of Violence* (New York: Routledge, 1989).

4. Sheila R. Herstein, *Mid-Victorian Feminist, Barbara Leigh Smith Bodichon*

(New Haven: Yale University Press, 1985), p. 35.

5. Candida Ann Lacey, introduction to *Barbara Leigh Smith Bodichon and the Langham Place Group* (New York: Routledge and Kegan Paul, 1987), p. 10.

6. Herstein, *Mid-Victorian Feminist*, p. 27.

7. Jane Lewis, *Women in England 1870–1950* (Bloomington, Ind.: Wheatsheaf, 1984), p. 3, quoted in Mary Lyndon Shanley, *Feminism, Marriage, and the Law in Victorian England, 1850–1895* (Princeton: Princeton University Press, 1989), p. 9.

8. Sir William Blackstone, *Commentaries on the Laws of England*, ed. J. DeWitt Andrews (Chicago: Callaghan and Co., 1899) bk I, ch. 15, §111, p. 442, quoted in Pateman, *The Sexual Contract*, p. 91.

9. Tristram Hutchinson and M. C. Merttins Swabey, *Reports of Cases Decided in the Court of Probate and in the Court for Divorce and Matrimonial Causes*, vol. 1 (London: Butterworths, 1860), p. 227.

10. In a case of criminal conversation, the husband charged another man with adultery with his wife. The suit's objective was to collect money from the adulterer for the husband's loss. The action could only be initiated by a husband, thus denoting that the wife was his property.

11. Herstein, *Mid-Victorian Feminist*, pp. 48–49.

12. Dorothy M. Stetson, *A Woman's Issue: The Politics of Family Law Reform in England* (Westport, Conn.: Green Wood, 1982) p. 33.

13. Pateman, *The Sexual Contract*, p. 121.

14. Barbara Leigh Smith Bodichon, "Remarks on Mill's *Political Economy*," unpublished notes, The Leigh Smith Papers, Girton College Library, quoted in Lacey, *Barbara Leigh Smith Bodichon*, p. 4.

15. Herstein, *Mid-Victorian Feminist*, p. 78.

16. Ibid., p. 192.

17. Bessie Rayner Parkes, "Barbara Leigh Smith Bodichon," *Englishwomen's Review* 210 (July 1891), p. 146, quoted in Shanley, *Feminism, Marriage, and the Law*, p. 32.

18. Barbara Leigh Smith Bodichon, "A Brief Summary, in Plain Language, of the Most Important Laws Concerning Women: Together with a Few Observations Thereon," in *Barbara Leigh Smith Bodichon*, p. 25–27.

19. Ibid., p. 31.

20. Elizabeth Gaskell, *The Life of Charlotte Brontë* (London: The Folio Society, 1971) p. 192.

21. Ibid., pp. 204, 277–78, 290.

22. Ibid., 130.

23. Carol Bock, *Charlotte Brontë and the Storyteller's Audience* (Iowa City:

University of Iowa Press, 1992), p. 30.

24. Irene Tayler, *Holy Ghosts: The Male Muses of Emily and Charlotte Brontë* (New York: Columbia University Press, 1990), p. 1.

25. Lyndall Gordon, *Charlotte Brontë: A Passionate Life* (New York: W. W. Norton & Co., 1994), p. 9.

26. Shuttleworth, *Charlotte Brontë*, p. 27.

27. Gaskell, *The Life of Charlotte Brontë* , pp. 116–17.

28. Shuttleworth, *Charlotte Brontë*, p. 19.

29. Gordon, *Charlotte Brontë*, pp. 143, 35.

30. Shuttleworth, *Charlotte Brontë*, p. 26–27.

31. Gaskell, *The Life of Charlotte Brontë* , pp. 132–33.

32. Marcelle Thiébaux, "Foucault's Fantasia for Feminists: The Woman Reading," in *Theory and Practice of Feminist Literary Criticism*, ed. Gabriela Mora and Karen S. Van Hooft (Ypsilanti: Bilingual Press, 1982), p. 48.

33. Gaskell, *The Life of Charlotte Brontë*, p. 239.

34. Elizabeth Rigby, "Review of *Jane Eyre* by Charlotte Brontë," *Quarterly Review* 84 (1848), p. 166.

35. I am indebted to Adrienne Rich's essay "Jane Eyre: The Temptations of a Motherless Woman," in *On Lies, Secrets, and Silence: Selected Prose 1966–1978* (New York: W. W. Norton, 1979) for providing the critical framework for my discussion of *Jane Eyre*.

36. Charlotte Brontë, *Jane Eyre* (Oxford: Clarendon, 1969), pp. 7–8. Subsequent references to this edition will be included parenthetically in the text.

37. Helene E. Roberts, "The Exquisite Slave: The Role of Clothes in the Making of the Victorian Woman," *Signs: Journal of Woman in Culture and Society* 2 (1977), p. 562.

38. Duncan Crow, *The Victorian Woman* (London: George Allen & Unwin, 1971), p. 120.

39. Roberts, "The Exquisite Slave," p. 555.

40. Judith Butler, *Gender Trouble: Feminism and the Subversion of Identity* (New York: Routledge, 1990), p. 22.

41. For further discussion of the oppression vs. empowerment controversy surrounding fashion, see *Fabrication: Costume and the Female Body*, eds. Jane Gaines and Charlotte Herzog (New York: Routledge, 1990); Stephen Kern, *Anatomy and Destiny: A Cultural History of the Human Body* (New York: Bobbs-Merrill Co., 1975); David Kunzle, "Dress Reform as Antifeminism: A Response to Helene E. Roberts's 'The Exquisite Slave: The Role of Clothes in the Making of the Victorian Woman,'" *Signs: Journal of Woman in Culture and Society* 2 (1977): 570–579; Helene E. Roberts, "Submission, Masochism,

Narcissism: Three Aspects of Women's Role as Reflected in Dress," in *Women's Lives: Perspectives on Progress and Change*," eds. Virginia Lussier and Joyce Wallstedt (Newark: University of Delaware, 1977); Valerie Steele, *Fashion and Eroticism: Ideals of Feminine Beauty from the Victorian Era to the Jazz Age* (New York: Oxford University Press, 1985); Thorstein Veblen, "Dress as an Expression of the Pecuniary Culture," in *The Theory of the Leisure Class* (New York: Random House, 1934); Iris Marion Young, "Women Recovering Our Clothes," in *Throwing Like A Girl and Other Essays in Feminist Philosophy and Social Theory* (Bloomington: Indiana University Press, 1990).

42. Rich, "Jane Eyre: The Temptations of a Motherless Woman," p. 96.

43. Ibid., p. 103.

44. Rather than noting the authorial and interpretative power that Jane gains through this marriage, Sharon Marcus writes than Jane transforms "herself into a prosthetic part" and "accedes to sovereignty through service." However, Marcus mistakenly writes that it is Rochester's right hand that cannot be restored, thus missing the significance of Jane becoming Rochester's "right hand." "The Profession of the Author: Abstraction, Advertising, and *Jane Eyre*," *PMLA* 110.2 (1995), p. 213.

45. Rich, "Jane Eyre: The Temptations of a Motherless Woman," p. 96.

46. Shuttleworth, *Charlotte Brontë*, p. 46.

CHAPTER FOUR
LUCY SNOWE AND THE POLITICS OF LOCATION

1. Charlotte Brontë, *Villette*, 2 vols. (New York: Alfred A. Knopf, 1992), 1:39. Subsequent references to this edition will be included parenthetically in the text.

2. Brenda R. Silver, "The Reflecting Reader in *Villette*," in *The Voyage In: Fictions of Female Development*, ed. Elizabeth Abel (Hanover: University Press of New England, 1983) p. 93.

3. For a discussion of Lucy as a deceitful, unreliable, or misleading narrator, see Mary Jacobus, "The Buried Letter: Feminism and Romanticism in *Villette*," *Women Writing and Writing About Women,* ed. Mary Jacobus (New York: Barnes & Noble, 1979): 42-60; Gregory S. O'Dea, "Narrator and Reader in Charlotte Brontë's *Villette*," *South Atlantic Review* 53 (1988): 41–57, and Nancy Sorkin Rabinowitz, "'Faithful Narrator' or 'Partial Eulogist': First-Person Narration in Brontë's *Villette*," *Journal of Narrative Technique* 16 (1985): 244–55.

4. For a different account of Polly Home, see Judith Lowder Newton, *Women, Power, and Subversion: Social Strategies in British Fiction, 1778–1860* (New York: Methuen, 1981): 86–124. In discussing Lucy's association of Polly with the "pampered spaniel," Newton writes that the association enforces the element of class protest but "ultimately this incipient protest, like the protest over women's sphere, is never developed" (118). However, if read as part of a series of comments regarding Polly beginning in Chapter 2, Vol. 1, Lucy not only suggests that Polly is a pampered member of the upper class, but consistently emphasizes her obsequious behavior as a woman.

5. Patricia S. Yaeger, "Honey-Mad Women: Charlotte Brontë's Bilingual Heroines," *Browning Institute Studies: An Annual of Victorian Literary and Cultural History* 14 (1986), p. 12.

6. Patricia E. Johnson, "'This Heretic Narrative': The Strategy of the Split Narrative in Charlotte Brontë's *Villette*," *Studies in English Literature, 1500–1900* 30 (1990), p. 621.

7. Ibid., p. 622.

8. Janet Freeman, "Looking on at Life: Objectivity and Intimacy in *Villette*," *Philological Quarterly* 67 (1988), p. 507.

9. Rachel Blau DuPlessis, *Writing Beyond the Ending: Narrative Strategies of Twentieth-Century Women Writers* (Bloomington: Indiana University Press, 1985), p. x.

10. Ibid., pp. 30, 21.

11. Ibid., p. 109.

12. I am especially indebted to Carol Bock for her discussion of Brontë's narrative method. See pp. 40–49 in *Charlotte Brontë and the Storyteller's Audience* (Iowa City: University of Iowa Press, 1992).

13. DuPlessis, *Writing Beyond the Ending*, pp. 11, 12.

14. Ibid., p. 126.

15. Elizabeth Gaskell, *The Life of Charlotte Brontë* (London: The Folio Society, 1971), p. 484.

16. Karen Lawrence, "The Cypher: Disclosure and Reticence in *Villette*," in *Critical Essays on Charlotte Brontë*, ed. Barbara Timm Gates (Boston: G. K. Hall, 1990), p. 308.

17. Harriet Martineau, "Review of *Villette* by Currer Bell," in *Critical Essays on Charlotte Brontë*, ed. Barbara Timm Gates (Boston: G. K. Hall, 1990), p. 154.

18. Sandra M. Gilbert and Susan Gubar, *The Madwoman in the Attic: The Woman Writer and the Nineteenth-Century Literary Imagination* (New Haven: Yale University Press, 1979), p. 400.

19. Rabinowitz, "'Faithful Narrator' or 'Partial Eulogist,'" p. 252.

20. Gilbert and Gubar, *The Madwoman in the Attic*, p. 425.

21. Linda C. Hunter, "Sustenance and Balm: The Question of Female Friendship in *Shirley* and *Villette*," *Tulsa Studies in Women's Literature* 1 (1982), p. 64.

22. Silver, "The Reflecting Reader," p. 111.

23. Christina Crosby, "Charlotte Brontë's Haunted Text," *Studies in English Literature 1500–1900* 24 (1984), p. 714–15.

24. M. M. Bakhtin, *The Dialogic Imagination*, trans. Caryl Emerson and Michael Holquist (Austin: University of Texas Press, 1981), p. 409.

25. Kate Millett, *Sexual Politics* (New York: Ballantine, 1969), p. 208.

26. Gaskell, *The Life of Charlotte Brontë*, p. 199.

CHAPTER FIVE
VIRGINIA WOOLF IN HER FATHER'S LIBRARY

1. Brenda R Silver, "What's Woolf Got to Do With It? or, The Perils of Popularity," *Modern Fiction Studies* 38 (1992), pp. 23–24.

2. In *All That Summer She Was Mad: Virginia Woolf: Female Victim of Male Medicine* (New York: Continuum, 1982), Stephen Trombley devotes a full chapter to each of the four doctors who attended or advised Woolf during her lifetime: Sir George Henry Savage, Sir Henry Head, Sir Maurice Craig, and T. B. Hyslop. In each chapter he discusses their diagnoses of madness, its causes and treatment along with each doctor's publications. Excepting Sir Henry Head, Trombley views their publications as political treatises and their diagnoses of insanity as moral judgments. On several occasions Trombley provides evidence of the medical profession's tendency to view itself as an agency for the enforcement of civil laws.

3. Virginia Woolf, *The Letters of Virginia Woolf*, ed. Nigel Nicolson and Joanne Trautmann, 6 vols. (New York: Harcourt Brace Jovanovich, 1975), 1:194. Subsequent references to this edition will be included parenthetically in the text according to volume and letter number.

4. Hermione Lee. *Virginia Woolf* (New York: Alfred A. Knopf, 1997), p. 179.

5. Charles E. Rosenberg, *No Other Gods: On Science and American Social Thought* (Baltimore: Johns Hopkins University Press, 1976), p. 54.

6. S. Weir Mitchell attended Jefferson Medical College from 1848–1850, and an examination of the medical textbooks on Jefferson's recommended reading list for those years reveals the sexist ideology permeating medical education. See, for example, the French medical textbook *A Treatise on the Diseased and Special Hygiene of Females,* written by Marc Colombat and translated by Charles D. Meigs (Philadelphia: Lea and Blanchard, 1845) and *Females and Their*

Diseases; A Series of Letters to His Class, written by Charles D. Meigs (Philadelphia: Lea and Blanchard, 1848).

7. Barbara Ehrenreich and Deirdre English, *Witches, Midwives, and Nurses: A History of Women Healers* (New York: The Feminist Press, 1973), p. 118.

8. S. Weir Mitchell, *Lectures on Diseases of the Nervous System, Especially in Women* (Philadelphia: Henry C. Lea's Son & Co., 1881), p. 228.

9. S. Weir Mitchell, *Fat and Blood: and How to Make Them* (Philadelphia: J. B. Lippincott & Co., 1877), pp. 48, 91.

10. Mitchell, *Fat and Blood*, p. 90.

11. Mitchell, *Doctor and Patient*, pp. 139–140.

12. Withers Moore, "The Higher Education of Women," *The British Medical Journal* 2 (1886), pp. 297, 296, 297.

13. Willoughby Francis Wade, "Ingleby Lectures on Some Functional Disorders of Females," *The British Medical Journal* 2 (1886), pp. 1053, 1095.

14. Theo B. Hyslop, "A Discussion on Occupation and Environment as Causative Factors of Insanity," *The British Medical Journal* 2 (1905), p. 942.

15. Virginia Woolf, *Three Guineas* (New York: Harcourt Brace Jovanovich, 1938), p. 166–68, n.38.

16. Quentin Bell, *Virginia Woolf: A Biography*, 2 vols. (New York: Harcourt Brace Jovanovich, 1972), 1:164.

17. Virginia Woolf, *Mrs. Dalloway* (London: Hogarth Press, 1963), p. 110.

18. Ann Douglas Wood, "The 'Fashionable Diseases': Women's Complaints and Their Treatment in Nineteenth-Century America," *Journal of Interdisciplinary History* 4 (1973) p. 39.

19. William Berkeley, *The Principles and Practice of Endocrine Medicine* (Philadelphia: Lea and Febiger, 1926), p. 295.

20. Leonard Woolf, *Beginning Again: An Autobiography of the Years 1911–1918* (London: Hogarth Press, 1964), p. 82.

21. In "A Sketch of the Past" Woolf wrote: "There was a slab outside the dining room door for standing dishes upon. Once when I was very small Gerald Duckworth lifted me onto this, and as I sat there he began to explore my body. I can remember the feel of his hand going under my clothes; going firmly and steadily lower and lower. I remember how I hoped that he would stop; how I stiffened and wriggled as his hand approached my private parts. But it did not stop. His hand explored my private parts too." See *Moments of Being*, ed. Jeanne Schulkind (New York: Harcourt Brace Jovanovich, 1985), p. 69. For other explicit references to the sexual abuse, see "22 Hyde Park Gate" in *Moments of Being*, 177; "Old Bloomsbury" in *Moments of Being* 181–82; a letter to Vanessa dated July 1911 (1:576), a letter to Vanessa dated February 1922

(2:1218); and a letter to Ethel Smyth dated January, 1941 (6:3678).

22. Roger Poole, *The Unknown Virginia Woolf* (New Jersey: Humanities Press, 1978); Louise DeSalvo, *Virginia Woolf: The Impact of Childhood Sexual Abuse on Her Life and Work* (New York: Ballantine, 1989).

23. Silver, "What's Woolf Got to Do With It?" p. 35.

24. The following are the complete footnotes as they appear in Quentin Bell's *Biography*: 1. "Statements by Leonard Woolf and the late Dr Noel Richards suggest that George's advances were made shortly after his mother's death; on the other hand unpublished memoirs (MH/A 14, 15 and 16) by Virginia make it almost certain that his activities began at, or were continued to, a much later date, i.e. 1903 or 1904. There is some reason to think that George's interest in Virginia was from the first peculiar: 'I still shiver with shame at the memory of my half-brother, standing me on a ledge, aged about 6 or so, exploring my private parts.' (VW to Ethel Smyth, 12 January 1941). Unusual behaviour for a young man in his twenties" (1:44). In this footnote Bell confuses the two Duckworth brothers. According to Woolf, it was Gerald, not George who abused her at the age of six (Cf with "A Sketch of the Past," p. 69). 2. "'George would fling himself on my bed, cuddling and kissing and otherwise embracing me in order, as he told Dr Savage later, to comfort me for the fatal illness of my Father—who was dying three or four storeys lower down of cancer.' (MH/A 16). I infer that the only people who could have told Savage of this were Vanessa or Virginia; the occasion must have been Virginia's madness in 1904. The only witness on whose evidence Savage would have spoken to George would have been Vanessa" (1:96).

25. Bell, *Virginia Woolf: A Biography*, 1:42.

26. Woolf, "22 Hyde Park Gate," *Moments of Being*, pp. 167, 166.

27. Bell, *Virginia Woolf: A Biography*, 1:44.

28. Ibid., 1:44.

29. DeSalvo, *Virginia Woolf*, pp. 32–33.

30. Ibid., pp. 21, 34.

31. Bell, *Virginia Woolf: A Biography*, 1:54.

32. Katherine C. Hill-Miller, "Leslie Stephen Revisited: A New Fragment of Virginia Woolf's 'A Sketch of the Past,'" in *Faith of a (Woman) Writer*, ed. Alice Kessler-Harris and William McBrien (New York: Greenwood Press, 1988), p. 282.

33. Lee, *Virginia Woolf*, pp. 140, 111.

34. Bell writes that in her diary Woolf kept a careful record of each book she read. For example, in 1897 between January 1 and June 30, she read the following: *Three Generations of English Women* (volumes 2 and 3); Froude's *Carlyle*,

Creighton's *Queen Elizabeth;* Lockhart's *Life of Sir Walter Scott; The Newcomes;* Carlyle's *Reminiscences; The Old Curiosity Shop; Essays in Ecclesiastical Biography* by James Stephen; *Felix Holt; John Halifax, Gentleman; Among My Books* and *My Study Windows; A Tale of Two Cities; Silas Marner; The Life of Coleridge; The Heart of Princess Osra;* three volumes of Pepys; Macaulay's *History; Barchester Towers;* a novel by Henry James; Carlyle's *French Revolution,* his *Cromwell* and *Life of Sterling;* a work by Lady Barlow; *Shirley;* Thomas Arnold's *History of Rome;* and *A Deplorable Affair* by W. E. Norris. *Virginia Woolf: A Biography,* 1:50–51.

35. George Eliot, *The George Eliot Letters,* ed. Gordon S. Haight, 9 vols. (New Haven: Yale University Press, 1954-78), 1:23.

36. Virginia Woolf, *The Voyage Out* (New York: Harcourt Brace Jovanovich, 1920), p. 46. Subsequent references to this edition will be included parenthetically in the text.

37. Woolf, *Moments of Being,* p. 70.

38. Ibid., p. 72.

39. V. N. Volosinov, *Marxism and the Philosophy of Language,* trans. Ladislav Matejka and I. R. Titunik (Cambridge: Harvard University Press, 1973), pp. 26, 37.

40. Ibid., p. 34.

41. Ibid., p. 36.

42. Ibid., p. 20.

43. Schulkind, Introduction, *Moments of Being,* p. 20.

44. Lee, *Virginia Woolf,* p. 464.

CHAPTER SIX
RACHEL'S VOYAGE OUT

1. Virginia Woolf, *The Voyage Out* (New York: Harcourt Brace Jovanovich, 1920), p. 187. Subsequent references to this edition will be included parenthetically in the text.

2. Marianne DeKoven, *Rich and Strange: Gender, History, Modernism* (Princeton: Princeton University Press, 1991), p. 132.

3. James Boswell, *Life of Johnson* (London: Oxford University Press, 1904), p. 327.

4. Louise DeSalvo, *Virginia Woolf's First Voyage: A Novel in the Making* (Totowa: Rowman and Littlefield, 1980), p. 126.

5. Ibid., pp. 138, 140.

6. Ibid., p. 7.

7. John Milton, "Comus," *John Milton: Complete Poems and Major Prose,* ed. Merritt Y. Hughes (Indianapolis: Odyssey Press, 1957), p. 110, ll 841–42.

8. Stephen Trombley, *All that Summer She Was Mad: Virginia Woolf: Female Victim of Male Medicine* (New York: Continuum, 1982), p. 33.

9. DeKoven, *Rich and Strange,* p. 128.

10. Mitchell A. Leaska, *The Novels of Virginia Woolf: From Beginning to End* (New York: John Jay Press, 1977), p. 38.

11. Madeline Moore, *The Short Season Between Two Silences: The Mystical and the Political in the Novels of Virginia Woolf* (Boston: George Allen & Unwin, 1984), p. 100.

12. Rosemary Pitt, "The Exploration of Self in Conrad's *Heart of Darkness* and Woolf's *The Voyage Out,"* *Conradiana* 10 (1978), p. 146.

13. Ibid., 149.

14. Elaine Scarry, *The Body in Pain: The Making and Unmaking of the World* (New York: Oxford, 1985), p. 254.

CHAPTER SEVEN

IN THE BREECHES, PETTICOATS AND PLEASURES OF *ORLANDO*

1. Quentin Bell, *Virginia Woolf: A Biography,* 2 vols. (New York: Harcourt Brace Jovanovich, 1972), 2:140.

2. Virginia Woolf, *A Writer's Diary,* ed. Leonard Woolf (New York: Harcourt Brace Jovanovich, 1953), pp. 157, 168.

3. Ibid., p. 131.

4. Virginia Woolf, *Orlando, A Biography* (New York: Harcourt Brace Jovanovich, 1928), p. 13. Subsequent references to this edition will be included parenthetically in the text.

5. J. J. Wilson, "Why *Orlando* Is Difficult?" in *New Feminist Essays on Virginia Woolf,* ed. Jane Marcus (Lincoln: University of Nebraska Press, 1981), p. 179.

6. Judy Little, "(En)gendering Laughter: Woolf's *Orlando* as Contraband in the Age of Joyce," *Women's Studies: An Interdisciplinary Journal* XV (1988), p. 183.

7. Majorie Garber, *Vested Interests: Cross-Dressing and Cultural Anxiety* (New York: HarperPerennial, 1993), p. 110.

8. Judith Butler, *Gender Trouble: Feminism and the Subversion of Identity* (New York: Routledge, 1990), p. 141.

9. Garber, *Vested Interests,* p. 10.

10. Ibid., p. 135.

11. Pamela Caughie, "Virginia Woolf's Double Discourse," in *Discontented Discourses: Feminism/Textual Intervention/Psychoanalysis*, ed. Marleen S. Barr and Richard Feldstein (Urbana: University of Illinois Press, 1989), p. 44.

12. Ibid., p. 46.

13. Garber, *Vested Interests*, p. 147.

14. Ibid., p. 17.

15. Makiko Minow-Pinkney, *Virginia Woolf and the Problem of the Subject* (New Brunswick: Rutgers University Press, 1987), p. 117.

16. Jean O. Love, "*Orlando* and Its Genesis: Venturing and Experimenting in Art, Love, and Sex," in *Virginia Woolf: Revaluation and Continuity*, ed. Ralph Freedman (Berkeley: University of California Press, 1980), p. 192.

17. Bell, *Virginia Woolf: A Biography*, 2:132, 138.

18. Nigel Nicolson, *Portrait of a Marriage* (New York: Athenaeum, 1973), p. 202.

19. Mitchell A. Leaska, *The Novels of Virginia Woolf: From Beginning to End* (New York: John Jay Press, 1977), p. xii.

20. Wilson, "Why *Orlando* Is Difficult?" p. 177.

21. Elizabeth Meese, "When Virginia Looked at Vita, What Did She See; or, Lesbian: Feminist: Woman—What's the Differ(e/a)nce?" *Feminist Studies* XVIII (1992), p. 111.

22. Sherron E. Knopp, "'If I saw you would you kiss me?' Sapphism and the Subversiveness of Virginia Woolf's *Orlando*," *PMLA* CIII (1988), p. 28.

23. Rachel Blau DuPlessis, *Writing Beyond the Ending, Narrative Strategies of Twentieth-Century Women Writers* (Bloomington: Indiana University Press, 1985), p. 62.

24. Caughie, "Virginia Woolf's Double Discourse," p. 42.

25. Garber, *Vested Interests*, p. 275.

26. Rosemary Jackson, *Fantasy: The Literature of Subversion* (New York: Routledge, 1981), p. 3.

27. Minow-Pinkney, *Virginia Woolf and the Problem of the Subject*, p. 119.

28. Butler, *Gender Trouble*, p. 148.

29. Michael Baker, the author of Radclyffe Hall's biography, does not characterize Virginia Woolf as supportive of Hall. See *On Three Selves: The Life of Radclyffe Hall* (New York: William Morrow, 1985): 229–230. However, over one hundred individuals were asked to speak in defense of *The Well of Loneliness*, and although Leonard and Vanessa were opposed to the idea, Virginia agreed to testify along with some forty others.

30. Michèle Aina Barale, "Below the Belt: (Un)Covering *The Well of Loneliness*," in *inside/out: Lesbian Theories, Gay Theories*, ed. Diana Fuss (New York: Routledge, 1991), p. 236.

31. Woolf, *A Writer's Diary*, p. 125.

32. Susan M. Squier, "Tradition and Revision in Woolf's *Orlando*: Defoe and 'The Jessamy Brides,'" *Women's Studies: An Interdisciplinary Journal* 12 (1986), p. 170.

33. Toril Moi, *Sexual/Textual Politics: Feminist Literary Theory* (New York: Methuen, 1985), p. 13.

34. Michel Foucault, *The History of Sexuality Volume I: An Introduction*, trans. Robert Hurley (New York: Vintage, 1978), p. 103.

35. Butler, *Gender Trouble*, p. 33.

36. Ibid., p. x.

EPILOGUE

1. Elizabeth Gaskell, *The Life of Charlotte Brontë* (London: The Folio Society, 1971), p. 259.

2. Gayatri Chakravorty Spivak, "Three Women's Texts and a Critique of Imperialism," in *"Race," Writing, and Difference*, ed. Henry Louis Gates, Jr. (Chicago: University of Chicago Press, 1985), p. 265, paraphrasing Elizabeth Fox-Genovese, "Placing Women's History in History," *New Left Review* 133 (May-June 1982), pp. 5–29.

3. Nancy Armstrong, *Desire and Domestic Fiction: A Political History of the Novel* (New York: Oxford University Press, 1987), p. 191.

4. Anita Levy, *Other Women: The Writing of Class, Race, and Gender, 1832–1898* (Princeton: Princeton University Press, 1991), pp. 8–18.

5. For a discussion of the two novels, see my "Dickens and Eliot in Dialogue: Empty Space, Angels and Maggie Tulliver," *The Victorian Newsletter* 80 (Fall 1991), pp. 18–23.

6. Elaine Showalter, *A Literature of Their Own: British Women Novelists From Brontë to Lessing* (Princeton: Princeton University Press, 1977), p. 13.

7. V. N. Volosinov, *Marxism and the Philosophy of Language*, trans. Ladislav Matejka and I. R. Titunik (Cambridge: Harvard University Press, 1973), p. 92.

8. Rachel Blau DuPlessis, *Writing Beyond the Ending: Narrative Strategies of Twentieth-Century Women Writers* (Bloomington: Indiana University Press, 1985), p. 30.

Selected Bibliography

Armstrong, Nancy. *Desire and Domestic Fiction: A Political History of The Novel.* Oxford: Oxford University Press, 1987.

Auerbach, Nina. "The Power of Hunger: Demonism and Maggie Tulliver." *Nineteenth Century Fiction* 30 (1975): 150–71.

Baker, Michael. *On Three Selves: The Life of Radclyffe Hall.* New York: William Morrow, 1985.

Baker, William. *The George Eliot—George Henry Lewes Library: An Annotated Catalogue of Their Books at Dr. Williams's Library, London.* New York: Garland, 1977.

———. "New George Eliot Letters." *The George Eliot Review* 23 (1992): 30–34.

Bakhtin, M. M. *The Dialogic Imagination*, trans. by Caryl Emerson and Michael Holquist. Austin: University of Texas Press, 1981.

Barale, Michèle Aina. "Below the Belt: (Un)Covering *The Well of Loneliness.*" In *inside/out: Lesbian Theories, Gay Theories*, ed. by Diana Fuss. New York: Routledge, 1991.

Barstow, Anne Llewellyn. *Witchcraze: A New History of the European Witch Hunts.* San Francisco: Pandora, 1994.

Barth, Karl. "An Introductory Essay." In *The Essence of Christianity*, by Ludwig Feuerbach. New York: Harper & Row, 1957.

Beer, Gillian. *George Eliot.* Brighton: Harvester Press, 1986.

Bell, Quentin. *Virginia Woolf: A Biography.* 2 vols. New York: Harcourt Brace Jovanovich, 1972.

Berkeley, William. *The Principles and Practice of Endocrine Medicine.* Philadelphia: Lea and Febiger, 1926.

Blackstone, Sir William. *Commentaries on the Laws of England*, ed. by J. DeWitt Andrews. Chicago: Callaghan and Co., 1899.

Bock, Carol. *Charlotte Brontë and the Storyteller's Audience.* Iowa City: University of Iowa Press, 1992.

Boswell, James. *Life of Johnson.* London: Oxford University Press, 1904.

Brady, Kristin. *George Eliot.* New York: St. Martin's Press, 1992.

Brontë, Charlotte. *Jane Eyre.* Oxford: Clarendon, 1969.

———. *Villette.* New York: Alfred A. Knopf, 1992.

Butler, Judith. *Gender Trouble: Feminism and the Subversion of Identity.* New York: Routledge, 1990.

Caughie, Pamela L. "Virginia Woolf's Double Discourse." In *Discontented Discourses: Feminism / Textual Intervention / Psychoanalysis,* ed. by Marleen S. Barr and Richard Feldstein. Urbana: University of Illinois Press.

Clark, Katerina and Michael Holquist. *Mikhail Bakhtin.* Cambridge: Harvard University Press, 1984.

Crosby, Christina. "Charlotte Brontë's Haunted Text." *Studies in English Literature 1500–1900* 24 (1984):701–715.

Crow, Duncan. *The Victorian Woman.* London: George Allen & Unwin Ltd, 1971.

Deegan, Thomas. "*Tractatus Theologico-Politicus.*" *George Eliot— George Henry Lewes Studies* 22–23 (1993): 1–16.

Defoe, Daniel. *The History of the Devil: Ancient and Modern in Two Parts.* Yorkshire: EP Publishing Limited, 1972.

DeKoven, Marianne. *Rich and Strange: Gender, History, Modernism.* Princeton: Princeton University Press, 1991.

DeSalvo, Louise. *Virginia Woolf's First Voyage: A Novel in the Making.* Totowa: Rowman and Littlefield, 1980.

———. *Virginia Woolf: The Impact of Childhood Sexual Abuse on Her Life and Work.* New York: Ballantine, 1989.

DuPlessis, Rachel Blau. *Writing Beyond the Ending: Narrative Strategies of Twentieth-Century Women Writers.* Bloomington: Indiana University Press, 1985.

Ehrenreich, Barbara and Deirdre English. *Witches, Midwives, and Nurses: A History of Women Healers.* New York: The Feminist Press, 1973.

Eliot, George. *The George Eliot Letters.* 9 vols. Ed. by Gordon S. Haight. New Haven: Yale University Press, 1954–1978.

———. *George Eliot: Selected Essays, Poems and Other* Writings, ed. by A. S. Byatt and Nicholas Warren. New York: Penguin, 1990.

———. *Middlemarch,* ed. by David R Carroll. Oxford: Clarendon, 1986.

———. *The Mill on the* Floss, ed. by Gordon Haight. Oxford: Clarendon, 1980.

Engels, Friedrich and Karl Marx. *The Marx-Engels* Reader, ed. by Robert C. Tucker. New York: W. W. Norton, 1978.

Ewen, C. L'Estrange. *Witchcraft and Demonianism.* London: Heath Cranton Limited, 1933.

Feuerbach, Ludwig. *The Essence of* Christianity, trans. by George Eliot. New York: Harper & Row, 1957.

Foucault, Michel. *The History of Sexuality Volume I: An Introduction,* trans. by Robert Hurley. New York: Vintage, 1978.

Fraiman, Susan. "*The Mill on the Floss,* the Critics, and the *Bildungsroman.*" *PMLA* 108 (1993): 136–150.

Fraser, Rebecca. *Charlotte Brontë.* London: Methuen, 1988.

Freeman, Janet. "Looking on at Life: Objectivity and Intimacy in *Villette.*" *Philological Quarterly* 67 (1988): 481–511.

Garber, Marjorie. *Vested Interests: Cross-Dressing and Cultural Anxiety.* New York: HarperPerennial, 1993.

Gaskell, Elizabeth. *The Life of Charlotte Brontë.* London: The Folio Society, 1971.

Gilbert, Sandra M. and Susan Gubar. *The Madwoman in the Attic: The Woman Writer and the Nineteenth-Century Literary Imagination.* New Haven: Yale University Press, 1979.

Gordon, Lyndall. *Charlotte Brontë: A Passionate Life.* New York: W. W. Norton & Co., 1994.

Haight, Gordon S. *George Eliot: A Biography.* New York: Penguin, 1968.

Harris, Horton. *David Friedrich Strauss and His Theology.* Cambridge: Cambridge University Press, 1973.

Heller, Deborah. "Tragedy, Sisterhood, and Revenge in *Corinne.*" *Papers on Language and Literature: A Journal for Scholars and Critics of Language and Literature* 26.2 (1990): 212–232.

Herstein, Sheila R. *Mid-Victorian Feminist, Barbara Leigh Smith Bodichon.* New Haven: Yale University Press, 1985.

Hill-Miller, Katherine C. "Leslie Stephen Revisited: A New Fragment of Virginia Woolf's 'A Sketch of the Past.'" In *Faith of a (Woman) Writer,* ed. by Alice Kessler-Harris and William McBrien. New York: Greenwood Press, 1988.

Homans, Margaret. "Eliot, Wordsworth, and the Scenes of the Sisters' Instruction." *Critical Inquiry* 8.2 (1981): 223–242.

Hunter, Linda C. "Sustenance and Balm: The Question of Female Friendship in *Shirley* and *Villette.*" *Tulsa Studies in Women's Literature* 1 (1982): 55–66.

Hutchinson, Tristram, D. C. L. and M. C. Merttins Swabey, D. C. L. Vol. 1 of *Reports of Cases Decided in the Court of Probate and in the Court for Divorce and Matrimonial Causes.* London: Butterworths, 1860.

Huxley, Leonard. *Life and Letters of Thomas Henry Huxley.* New York: D. Appleton, 1900.

Hyslop, Theo. B., M.D. "A Discussion on Occupation and Environment as Causative Factors of Insanity." *The British Medical Journal* 2 (1905): 941–45.

Jackson, Rosemary. *Fantasy: The Literature of Subversion.* New York: Routledge, 1981.

Jacobus, Mary. "The Buried Letter: Feminism and Romanticism In *Villette.*" In *Women Writing and Writing About Women*, ed. by Mary Jacobus. New York: Barnes & Noble, 1979.

———. "The Question of Language: Men of Maxims and *The Mill on the Floss.*" *Critical Inquiry* 8.2 (1981): 207–222.

Johnson, Patricia E. "'This Heretic Narrative': The Strategy of the Split Narrative in Charlotte Brontë's *Villette.*" *Studies in English Literature, 1500–1900* 30 (1990): 617–631.

Knopp, Sherron E. "'If I saw you would you kiss me?' Sapphism and the Subversiveness of Virginia Woolf's *Orlando*" *PMLA* 103 (1988): 24–34.

Krämer, Heinrich and James Sprenger. *The Malleus Maleficarum*, trans. by Montague Summers. New York: Dover Publications, 1971.

Lacey, Candida Ann, ed. *Barbara Leigh Smith Bodichon and the Langham Place Group.* New York: Routledge and Kegan Paul, 1987.

Laqueur, Thomas. Introduction to *The Making of the Modern Body: Sexuality and Society in the Nineteenth Century*, ed. by Catherine Gallagher and Thomas Laqueur. Berkeley: University of California Press, 1987.

Lawrence, Karen. "The Cypher: Disclosure and Reticence in *Villette.*" In *Critical Essays on Charlotte Brontë*, ed. by Barbara Timm Gates. Boston: G. K. Hall, 1990.

Leaska, Mitchell A. *The Novels of Virginia Woolf: From Beginning to End.* New York: John Jay Press, 1977.

———. "Virginia Woolf's *The Voyage Out:* Character Deduction and the Function of Ambiguity." *Virginia Woolf Quarterly* 1.2 (1973): 18–41.

Lee, Hermione. *Virginia Woolf.* New York: Alfred A. Knopf, 1997.

Levy, Anita. *Other Women: The Writing of Class, Race, and Gender, 1832–1898.* Princeton: Princeton University Press, 1991.

Lewis, Jane. *Women in England 1870–1950.* Bloomington: Wheatsheaf, 1984.

Little, Judy. "(En)gendering Laughter: Woolf's *Orlando* as Contraband in the Age of Joyce." *Women's Studies: An Interdisciplinary Journal* 15 (1988): 179–191.

Love, Jean. O. "*Orlando* and Its Genesis: Venturing and Experimenting in Art, Love, and Sex." In *Virginia Woolf: Revaluation and Continuity*, ed. by Ralph Freedman. Berkeley: University of California Press, 1980.

Marcus, Sharon. "The Profession of the Author: Abstraction, Advertising, and *Jane Eyre.*" *PMLA* 110.2 (1995): 206–19.

Martineau, Harriet. "Review of *Villette* by Currer Bell." In *Critical Essays on Charlotte Brontë*, ed. by Barbara Timm Gates. Boston: G. K. Hall, 1990. 253–256.

Massey, Marilyn Chapin. *Christ Unmasked: The Meanings of The Life of Jesus in German Politics.* Chapel Hill: University of North Carolina Press, 1983.

Meese, Elizabeth. "When Virginia Looked at Vita, What Did She See; or, Lesbian: Feminist: Woman—What's the Differ(e/a)nce?" *Feminist Studies* 18 (1992): 99–117.

Miller, Nancy K. "Emphasis Added: Plots and Plausibilities in Women's Fiction." *PMLA* 96.1 (1981): 36–48.

Millett, Kate. *Sexual Politics.* New York: Ballantine, 1969.

Minow-Pinkney, Makiko. *Virginia Woolf and the Problem of the Subject.* New Brunswick: Rutgers University Press, 1987.

Mitchell, S. Weir. *Doctor and Patient.* Philadelphia: J. B. Lippincott, 1888.

———. *Fat and Blood: And How To Make Them.* Philadelphia: J. B. Lippincott & Co., 1877.

———. *Lectures on Diseases of the Nervous System, Especially in Women.* Philadelphia: Henry C. Lea's Son & Co., 1881.

Moi, Toril. *Sexual Textual Politics.* New York: Methuen, 1985.

Moore, Madeline. *The Short Season Between Two Silences: The Mystical and the Political in the Novels of Virginia Woolf.* Boston: George Allen & Unwin, 1984.

——. "Some Female Versions of Pastoral: *The Voyage Out* and Matriarchal Mythologies." In *New Feminist Essays on Virginia Woolf,* ed. by Jane Marcus. Lincoln: University of Nebraska Press, 1981.

Moore, Withers. "The Higher Education of Women." *The British Medical Journal* 2 (1886): 295–299.

Nicolson, Nigel. *Portrait of a Marriage.* New York: Athenaeum, 1973.

Pateman, Carole. *The Sexual Contract.* Stanford: Stanford University Press, 1988.

Peterson, Carla L. *The Determined Reader: Gender and Culture in the Novel from Napoleon to Victoria.* New Brunswick: Rutgers University Press, 1986.

Pitt, Rosemary. "The Exploration of Self in Conrad's *Heart of Darkness* and Woolf's *The Voyage Out.*" *Conradiana* 10 (1978): 141–54.

Poole, Roger. *The Unknown Virginia Woolf.* New Jersey: Humanities Press, 1978.

Poovey, Mary. *Uneven Development: The Ideological Work of Gender in Mid-Victorian England.* Chicago: University of Chicago Press, 1988.

Rabinowitz, Nancy Sorkin. "'Faithful Narrator' or 'Partial Eulogist': First-Person Narration in Brontë's *Villette.*" *Journal of Narrative Technique* 15 (1985): 244–255.

Rigby, Elizabeth. Rev. of *Jane Eyre* by Charlotte Brontë. *Quarterly Review* 84 (1848): 162–176.

Roberts, Helene E. "The Exquisite Slave: The Role of Clothes in the Making of the Victorian Woman." *Signs: Journal of Woman in Culture and Society* 2 (1977): 554–569.

Rosen, Barbara. *Witchcraft.* New York: Taplinger, 1972.

Rosenberg, Charles E. *No Other Gods: On Science and American Social Thought.* Baltimore: Johns Hopkins University Press, 1976.

Russell, Jeffrey B. *A History of Witchcraft: Sorcerers, Heretics and Pagans.* London: Thames and Hudson, 1980.

Scarry, Elaine. *The Body in Pain: The Making and Unmaking of the World.* New York: Oxford, 1985.

Schiebinger, Londa. "Skeletons in the Closet: The First Illustrations of the Female Skeleton in Eighteenth-Century Anatomy." In *The Making of the Modern Body: Sexuality and Society in the Nineteenth Century,* ed. by Catherine Gallagher and Thomas Laqueur. Berkeley: University of California Press, 1987.

Scott, Walter. *Letters on Demonology and Witchcraft.* East Ardsley, Wakefield, England: S. R. Publishers, 1968.

Shanley, Mary Lyndon. *Feminism, Marriage, and the Law in Victorian England, 1850–1895.* Princeton: Princeton University Press, 1989.

Showalter, Elaine. *A Literature of Their Own: British Women Novelists from Brontë to Lessing.* Princeton: Princeton University Press, 1977.

Shuttleworth, Sally. *Charlotte Brontë and Victorian Psychology.* Cambridge: Cambridge University Press, 1996.

Silver, Brenda R. "The Reflecting Reader in *Villette.*" In *The Voyage In: Fictions of Female Development,* ed. by Elizabeth Abel. Hanover: University Press of New England, 1983.

——. "What's Woolf Got to Do With It? or, The Perils of Popularity." *Modern Fiction Studies* 38 (1992): 21–60.

Spender, Dale. *Mothers of the Novel: 100 Good Women Writers Before Jane Austen.* London: Pandora, 1986.

Spivak, Gayatri. "Three Women's Texts and a Critique of Imperialism." In *"Race" Writing, and Difference,* ed. by Henry Louis Gates, Jr. Chicago: University of Chicago Press, 1985.

Squier, Susan M. "Tradition and Revision in Woolf's *Orlando*: Defoe and 'The Jessamy Brides.'" *Women's Studies: An Interdisciplinary Journal* 12 (1986): 167–178.

Staël, Madame de. *Corinne, or Italy,* trans. by Avriel H. Goldberger. New Brunswick: Rutgers University Press, 1987.

Stetson, Dorothy M. *A Woman's Issue: The Politics of Family Law Reform in England.* Westport, Conn.: Green Wood, 1982.

Strauss, David. *The Life of Jesus, Critically Examined,* trans. by Marian Evans. Vol. 1 & 2. New York: Calvin Blanchard, 1970.

Tayler, Irene. *Holy Ghosts: The Male Muses of Emily and Charlotte Brontë.* New York: Columbia University Press, 1990.

Thiébaux, Marcelle. "Foucault's Fantasia for Feminists: The Woman Reading." In *Theory and Practice of Feminist Literary Criticism*, ed. by Gabriela Mora and Karen S. Van Hooft. Ypsilanti: Bilingual Press, 1982.

Thomas à Kempis. *The Imitation of Christ*, ed. by Ernest Rhys. London: J. M. Dent, 1910.

Trombley, Stephen. *All That Summer She Was Mad: Virginia Woolf: Female Victim of Male Medicine*. New York: Continuum, 1982.

Veith, Ilza. *Hysteria, The History of a Disease*. Chicago: University of Chicago Press, 1965.

Vlasopolos, Anca. "Shelley's Triumph of Death in Virginia Woolf's *Voyage Out*." *Modern Language Quarterly* 47.2 (1986): 130–153.

Volosinov, V. N. *Marxism and the Philosophy of Language*, trans. by Ladislav Matejka and I. R. Titunik. Cambridge: Harvard University Press, 1973.

Wade, Willoughby Francis. "Ingleby Lectures on Some Functional Disorders of Females." *The British Medical Journal* 2 (1886): 1053–1056, 1095–1096, 1154–1156.

Wilson, J. J. "Why *Orlando* Is Difficult?" In *New Feminist Essays on Virginia Woolf*, ed. by Jane Marcus. Lincoln: University of Nebraska Press, 1981.

Wood, Ann Douglas. "The 'Fashionable Diseases': Women's Complaints and their Treatment in Nineteenth-Century America." *Journal of Interdisciplinary History* 4 (1973): 25–52.

Woolf, Leonard. *Beginning Again: An Autobiography of the Years 1911–1918*. London: Hogarth Press, 1964.

Woolf, Virginia. *The Diary of Virginia Woolf*. Vol. III. Ed. by Anne Olivier Bell. London: Hogarth Press, 1978.

———. *The Letters of Virginia* Woolf, ed. by Nigel Nicolson and Joanne Trautmann. New York: Harcourt Brace Jovanovich, 1975.

———. *Moments of* Being, ed. by Jeanne Schulkind. New York: Harcourt Brace Jovanovich, 1985.

———. *Mrs. Dalloway*. London: Hogarth Press, 1963.

———. *Orlando: A Biography*. New York: Harcourt Brace Jovanovich, 1928.

———. *A Room of One's Own*. New York: Harcourt Brace Jovanovich, 1929.

———. *Three Guineas*. New York: Harcourt Brace Jovanovich, 1938.

——. *The Voyage Out.* New York: Harcourt Brace Jovanovich, 1920.

——. *A Writer's* Diary, ed. by Leonard Woolf. New York: Harcourt Brace Jovanovich, 1953.

Yaeger, Patricia S. "Honey-Mad Women: Charlotte Brontë's Bilingual Heroines." *Browning Institute Studies: An Annual of Victorian Literary and Cultural History* 14 (1986): 11–35.

Index

agency, ix, 1, 8, 9, 21, 30, 57, 63, 71, 87, 137
Anti-Slavery Convention, 51
Armstrong, Nancy, 50, 137
Auerbach, Nina, 29

Baker, William, 14
Bakhtin, Mikhail, ix, 3
Barale, Michèle Aina, 134
Barry, William, 29
Bedford College, 50
Bell, Quentin, 96, 98–100, 119, 132, 156 n.24 & 34
Berkeley, William, 97
biblical criticism, 14
Blackwood's Magazine, 24
Blackwood, John, 25
Bodichon, Barbara Leigh Smith, 19, 53
body, 4, 36, 41, 59, 62, 76, 78, 91, 93, 94, 104, 107, 122, 135, 137, 139, 140
Bostock v. Bostock, 51
Brady, Kristin, 29
Bray, Charles, 29
Brontë Household, 56
Brontë, Charlotte, ix, 3, 5, 8, 50, 71, 89, 137, 139
and books, 55–58
and Brussels, 58
and marriage, 54
female friendship, 63, 66
Jane Eyre, ix, 9, 49, 50, 58–69, 80, 83, 137
Villette, 9, 71–87, 124
Brontë, Emily, 56
Brontë, Patrick, 56, 82
Butler, Judith, 3, 4, 5, 6, 7, 62, 129, 136
Byatt, A. S., 23

Calvinism, 23, 27, 31, 63, 65
Caughie, Pamela L., 131
Chapman, John, 18
classical education, 6, 30
Corinne, or Italy (Staël), 42–43
coverture, 51
Crosby, Christina, 85
Crow, Duncan, 61

Daily News, The, 15, 24
Deegan, Thomas, 13
DeKoven, Marianne, 120
DeSalvo, Louise, 98, 100, 101, 118
Desire and Domestic Fiction (Armstrong), 137
Diana of the Crossways (Meredith), 52
Dickens, Charles, 13, 138, 160
discourse, ix, 3–7, 10, 12, 27, 36, 41, 45, 57, 98, 107, 121, 135, 139, 140
discursive agency, 3, 6, 9, 47, 107, 139. *See also* agency
Dombey and Son (Dickens), 138
domestic romance, 71, 80
double-voiced discourse, 75
Duckworth, George, 98–100, 156 n.24
Duckworth, Gerald, 98, 155 n.21, 156 n.24
Duncan, Matthews, 6
DuPlessis, Rachel Blau, 80, 133, 139

Ehrenreich, Barbara, 92
Eliot, George, ix, 3, 5, 8, 11, 22, 29, 53, 73, 89, 104, 138, 139
"Address to Working Men, By Felix Holt," 24
"Margaret Fuller and Mary Wollstonecraft," 27
"The Influence of Rationalism," 31, 33
"The Natural History of German Life," 22, 24
Adam Bede, 15
Daniel Deronda, 15
George Eliot Letters, The, 11, 71, 138, 148 n.27
Middlemarch, 15
Mill on the Floss, The, 8, 30, 34–47, 138
Silas Marner, 15

Engels, Friedrich, 16, 18, 22, 23, 26
English, Deirdre, 92
Ermarth, Elizabeth, 13
Essence of Christianity, The
   (Feuerbach), 16

Feuerbach, Ludwig, 13, 14, 16, 21
Foucault, Michel, 3, 4, 5, 7
Fraiman, Susan, 29
Freeman, Janet, 80
Freiligrath, Ferdinand, 18

Garber, Majorie, 125, 130, 131
Gaskell, Elizabeth, 56, 82, 86
gender, 5, 125, 127, 140
gender trouble, 78, 128
German higher criticism, 13, 14, 24,
   139
Gilbert, Sandra M., 29, 82, 83
Gordon, Lyndall, 57
Gosse, Edmund, 29
Gothic romance, 71, 80
Gubar, Susan, 29, 82, 83
Gulliver's Travels (Swift), 59
Gutwirth, Madelyn, 43

Haight, Gordon, 12, 13, 14, 18, 27,
   29
Hall, Radclyffe, 134
Harris, Horton, 14
Hegelians, 14, 15
Heller, Deborah, 43
Hennell, Charles, 15
Hennell, Sara Sophia, 13
heterosexism, 63
History of Rome (Goldsmith), 8, 56,
   59
History of the Devil, The (Defoe), 8,
   30, 33, 34–36, 37, 46, 146 *n*.8
Homans, Margaret, 30
Hunter, Linda C., 84
Huxley, T. H., 18, 24
Hyslop, T. B., 93–94, 97, 122, 154
   n.2

Ibsen, Henrik, 8, 121
Imitation of Christ, The (Thomas à
   Kempis), 8,19, 30, 39–41, 46, 57,
   148 *n*.26 & 27
incest, 90

Jackson, Rosemary, 134
Jacobus, Mary, 30, 47, 152 *n*.3

Knopp, Sherron E., 133

Laqueur, Thomas, 2
Lawrence, Karen, 82
Leaska, Mitchell, 120, 132
*Letters on Demonology and
   Witchcraft,* (Scott), 31
Levy, Anita, 137–38
Lewes, George Henry, 14
Lewis, Maria, 11
Little, Judy, 124
Love, Jean O., 132

Malleus Maleficarum, The (Kramer
   and Sprenger), 32
Marx, Karl, 8, 13, 17–27
Massey, Marilyn, 14
materialism, 16, 18, 22
Mazzini, 18
Meese, Elizabeth, 133
Meredith, George, 52
Miller, Nancy K., 30
Millett, Kate, 84
Milton, John, 34, 56, 57, 58, 118
Minow-Pinkney, Makiko, 132, 134
misogyny, 6, 32, 33, 36, 47
Mitchell, S. Weir, 90, 91–92, 94, 95,
   97, 101, 122, 154 *n*.6
Moi, Toril, 135
Moore, Withers, 2, 93, 94
Mott, Lucretia Coffin, 51

Nicolson, Nigel, 99–100, 132
Norton, Caroline Sheridan, 52
novelistic discourse, 3, 5, 17, 23, 27,
   58, 106, 138

*Other Women: The Writing of Class,
   Race, and Gender, 1832–1898*
   (Levy), 137
Owen, Richard, 18

Pamela (Richardson), 137
Pateman, Carole, 49
patriarchy, 59, 65, 73, 94, 98
politics of location, 9, 71, 72
Poole, Roger, 98, 119
Poovey, Mary, 6

Queen's College, 50, 93

Rabinowitz, Nancy Sorkin, 83, 152 *n.*3
Radcliff, 2
rest cure, 90, 91–92, 95, 96, 122
Rich, Adrienne, 64, 66, 67
Rigby, Elizabeth, 49, 59
Roberts, Helene, 61
romance, ix, 42, 50, 54, 59, 64, 71, 73, 75, 80, 82, 95, 111, 139
romance plot, ix, 68, 130, 140
romantic love, 9, 43, 46, 47, 65, 82, 109, 117, 136
Rosenberg, Charles E., 91
Russell, Jeffrey B., 32

Sackville-West, Vita, 98, 132, 133
Savage, George Henry, 96, 97
Scarry, Elaine, 122
scenes of reading, ix, 3, 6, 8, 9, 27, 30, 36, 50, 59, 104, 139, 141
Schiebinger, Londa, 1
Schreiner, Olive, 139
Schulkind, Jeanne, 107
Scott, Walter, 7, 11, 12, 31, 73
sexuality, 5, 9, 29, 99, 114, 119, 131, 135
Showalter, Elaine, 2, 138
Shuttleworth, Sally, 50, 56
Silver, Brenda R., 72, 84, 89, 90
Spencer, Herbert, 23
Spender, Dale, 2
Spinoza, 13
Spivak, Gayatri, 50, 137
Squier, Susan M., 135
Staël, Madame de, 43
Stanton, Elizabeth Cady, 51
Stephen, Laura, 100
Story of an African Farm, The (Schreiner), 139
Strauss, David, 13, 14, 21
subversive repetition, 3, 67, 83, 107, 127, 131, 138, 140
Swift, Jonathan, 59
swimming test, 8, 31, 33, 34

Tayler, Irene, 56
Thiébaux, Marcelle, 57
Thomas à Kempis, 8, 19, 21, 30, 39–41, 42, 44, 47, 57, 148 *n.*26 & 27

Victorian dress, 61
Victorian marriage, 50–54
Volosinov, V. N., 106, 107, 138

Wade, Francis, 93, 94
Watt, Ian, 2
Waverley (Scott), 11
Westminster Review, 18
Wilson, J. J., 124, 132
witches, 8, 29, 30, 32–33
Wood, Ann Douglas, 97
Woolf, Leonard, 97, 98
Woolf, Virginia, ix, 3, 5, 9, 10, 29, 89, 139
  and books, 101–4
  and incest, 97–101
  and the rest cure, 96
  Moments of Being, 107
  Mrs. Dalloway, 96
  Orlando, 9, 123–136
  The Voyage Out, 9, 104, 106, 110–122
  Three Guineas, 95
  To the Lighthouse, 119, 123
Wordsworth, William, 12, 13

Yaeger, Patricia S., 76

W·R·I·T·I·N·G A·B·O·U·T W·O·M·E·N
Feminist Literary Studies

This is a literary series devoted to feminist studies on past and contemporary women authors, exploring social, psychological, political, economic, and historical insights directed toward an interdisciplinary approach.

The series is dedicated to the memory of Simone de Beauvoir, an early pioneer in feminist literary theory.

Persons wishing to have a manuscript considered for inclusion in the series should submit a letter of inquiry, including the title and a one-page abstract of the manuscript to the general editor:

Professor Esther K. Labovitz
Department of English
Pace University
Pace Plaza
New York, NY 10038
(212) 488-1416